S0-BRO-069

THE ANGLICAN DILEMMA

BY THE SAME AUTHOR

The Middle Ages in the West
Judgement Reserved
The Law (*Heritage Series*)
The Judicial Office and Other Matters
A History of the Liberal Party
Order and Disorder
The Administration of the Law

The Pastured Shire (*Verses*)

THE
ANGLICAN DILEMMA

by

THE RIGHT HONOURABLE
SIR HENRY SLESSER, P.C.

"The idea of worship is different in the Catholic Church
from the idea of it in Anglicanism; for, in truth, the
religions are different . . . they differ in kind, not in degree."

CARDINAL NEWMAN in *Loss and Gain*

HUTCHINSON
Stratford Place
London

120178 283 √
5ℓ28

Hutchinson & Co. (Publishers) Ltd.
London, New York, Melbourne, Sydney, Cape Town

First published 1952

Printed in Great Britain
by The Anchor Press, Ltd.,
Tiptree, Essex

To my nephew
ARTHUR GRANT

CONTENTS

INTRODUCTORY

Lest any reader of this book may be misled as to its purpose, I would wish to say at the outset that it represents the conclusions at which I have arrived after careful and protracted study whether a convinced Catholic can in conscience remain within the Anglican communion. It is my hope, therefore, that no one will think that I have written in malice; I recognize the work which the Anglicans have done in the past, more particularly in the social sphere, but I must agree, possibly with the majority of them, that their Church, the more closely it is examined, emerges as a Protestant institution.

H. S.

Postbridge,
Dartmoor, Devon,
March, 1952.

PREFACE

THE Church of England (which some of its members claim to be both Catholic and Reformed) is, by common consent, a national institution. It possesses therefore that prestige and dignity which of necessity pertains to a society which purports to speak in matters spiritual for the whole nation, which solemnly crowns her Sovereign, whose Bishops alone are recognized in law as possessing a specific precedence, a place in the legislature and status; its ministers being accorded the style and privilege of "clerks in holy orders". To these advantages is added a pretension to unbroken antiquity supported by the possession of ancient Catholic cathedrals and other fabrics and titles, which is not without its impressive effect on those ignorant of history. Thus, one example of many, in April 1093 the Cathedral Church of Winchester was consecrated and, in 1893, the eight-hundredth anniversary of that event was there commemorated.

"Where," rhetorically asked the Dean, "would be found a better symbol of the continuity and the corporate life of the Church of England than in the record of eight hundred years during which our countrymen had worshipped there? No one who has learned to prize liturgical worship can without emotion remember that the prayers he hears today have been heard by myriads of Churchmen of preceding generations not only in England, but in other parts of Christendom. An event like this brings the thought home in a deeply significant and forcible manner, and we may feel certain that the Churchmen of Winchester diocese realised then, as they never realised before, how the ancient liturgy has preserved the faith in their own portion of England, and how deep are the roots which the Church has struck into our national life."

That St. Birinus, the "Apostle of Wessex", was sent by the advice and authority of Pope Honorius I to the West Saxons and that another Honorius, Archbishop of Canterbury (627–655), "by the authority of the papal precept", ordained the first Bishop of the West Saxons, while the present Anglican one has to declare that the Pope "hath no jurisdiction in England", need not detain us. The fact is that the continuity of the episcopal title and the retention of Catholic shrines by Anglicans have persuaded large numbers that the present Archbishop of Canterbury, for instance, "sits in the chair of St. Augustine", whereas in order to hold his metropolitan see he must repudiate and abjure the pontifical master of whom St. Augustine and his successors (including Cranmer) were to a great extent delegates.

But whether this alleged historical continuity be believed or not—and modern knowledge is making its acceptance increasingly difficult[1]—the fact remains that the Church which bears the challenging title of "National" in reality commands the allegiance of about five per cent of the total population of England. According to recent researches the number of professed Christians in England who attend any place of worship is about a tenth of the population, of which not more than a half may be said to be Anglican. A clergyman with experience in industrial areas reckons the church-goers among the workers, however, as about one in forty; all the others being made up of the middle classes. The figures available as to church attendance provided by Rowntree and Lavers in their statistics affecting the metropolitan city of York in 1948 confirm these estimates. Their census is based on attendances at two Sundays and discloses that the number fell from 7453 in 1901 to 3384 in 1948, the adult population in the interval having risen from 48,000 in 1901 to 78,500 in 1948 (that is, persons of 17 or over). The number of

---

[1] Nevertheless similar claims are still constantly made; one of the last being at the Commemoration of St. Aidan in 1951. "The Church of England is the ancient Catholic Church of this land," writes the present Archbishop of York (*The Claims of the Church of England*, Garbett).

church-goers of all denominations had thus fallen considerably.

By way of comparison it is also stated that of these the Anglican had fallen from 43 per cent to 33, while the Catholic increased from 13 to 30 per cent. Nonconformity declined less than the Anglicans. "It is indeed startling," write the authors, "that in an archiepiscopal city the total attendance is less than that of the free churches, and only 10 per cent more than the attendances at the Roman Catholic churches." Moreover, "the proportion of younger adults attending Catholic churches is substantially higher than the proportion in the nation as a whole". At High Wycombe, however, the Nonconformist outnumbered considerably the Catholic and Anglicans, though the latter were only one per cent higher than the Catholics. There is no reason to suppose that the proportion of worshippers in other parts of England shows any marked difference from these figures; that is to say, taking a half of the attendances as Anglican, they represent, as has been said, not more than a twentieth of the English people.[1]

Leaving aside statistics, which at best are but approximate, we ask the question, Why, when the Church of England was still so relatively strong a hundred years ago, has she lost the greater part of the population, not to other denominations, but to an indifferent agnosticism?

It is suggested that the pursuit of "comprehensiveness", so long the solace of Anglican apologists, has been her particular bane, one not so much affecting Nonconformists, and Catholics not at all. An Anglican cleric today, apparently, may believe as he will whether the Scriptures are true, whether Christ was born of a Virgin, whether there was a physical Resurrection, whether Hell exists or the conditions of eternal damnation, whether miracles are possible and whether the Church is a visible mystical body or not. He is free to accept varying and contradictory doctrines as to the nature of

---

[1] In 1934, when the population was a quarter less than it is today, there were 21,000 Anglican clergy. Today there are fewer than 15,000. Infant baptisms declined from 525,835 in 1947 to 450,611 in 1950, though there was an increase of about 1000 in adults; 8946 in all.

Baptism and of the Eucharist, and, if he wishes, to advocate
Divorce, Euthanasia or Eugenics. He may, but need not,
practise Confession and may or may not regard his Bishop as
having apostolical succession (a doubt which may be shared
by the Bishop himself).[1] Indeed the only matter on which an
Anglican clergyman is very definitely required to have a clear
view is as to the untenable nature of the claims of the Papacy; a
very negative foundation on which to base an official national
religion. Nevertheless, a large number of Anglicans rejoice
in this latitude, among them, apparently, the present Archbishop of Canterbury, who, in his introduction to the very
important report on *Catholicity* presented to him in 1947 by
some of the most learned members of his Church, declared that
the Church over which he presides should and ought to
include "many varieties of function, practice and theological
emphasis". On the other hand, the signatories themselves
collectively warn their co-religionists that

> "Today it is only too apparent that, notwithstanding the
> genuine achievements of Anglican synthesis, the forces of
> disintegration are strong. There are those who, virtually
> omitting the doctrine of the Church from its place in the
> Gospel, replace it by a doctrine of the spiritual vocation of
> the English community. There are, on the other hand,
> those who are content to practise an introverted and
> pietistic ecclesiasticism under the name of 'Catholic'
> churchmanship. There are those who, intent upon the idea
> of Christian leadership in the march of progress, have
> twisted the Gospel into a sort of pragmatist panacea for
> human ills, instead of a Gospel of God's *truth*, which makes
> its demands upon mankind just because it is true. There
> are, on the other hand, those who in their eagerness to

[1] Canon Collins, Chancellor of St. Paul's Cathedral, has recently stated that
his Church makes "the gravest possible error in demanding that a person, in
order to be a member of the Church of England, must subscribe to the creeds",
and again "To allow them to become a test, a barrier, for the life of fellowship
within the Church was, he believed, madness."

preach Divine Redemption ignore (as does the Report on
the *Conversion of England*) the doctrine of Creation which is
its groundwork. The fulness of our tradition is often far
to seek, and it is idle to be content that the Church of
England includes a 'rich variety', if that variety represents
distortion and fragmentation of the truth."

To the same effect wrote Mr. Dark, the late editor of
the Anglo-Catholic *Church Times*:

"I do not share the satisfaction, apparently felt by practically all the bishops, that the English Church is comprehensive, nor do I believe that it must always have a place in
its ranks for Catholics, Modernists and extreme Protestants.
The advantages of comprehension were first preached by
Dean Stanley, although Queen Elizabeth, who had no
particular religion of her own, certainly intended the
English Church to be comprehensive. Dean Stanley would
have had things go farther than they have yet gone, and by
giving Communion in Westminster Abbey to a Unitarian
minister, he suggested that the English Church should be
as comprehensive as the British Empire."

Yet, as has been said by another Anglican, Cecilia Ady:

"The Church of England is a typically English institution—its ideal of comprehensiveness and the ambiguities
discernible in its doctrinal and constitutional position have
the effect of encouraging every individual member, *so far
as he thinks about it at all*, to place his own interpretation
upon it. According to the point of view from which it is
regarded, it is at once a part of the ancient church of
Christendom and a product of the Protestant reformation, a
department of state and a society possessing inherent independence, a religious body belonging to England alone
and a member of a world-wide communion."

The authoress, in approving apparently this medley of confusion, represents a large part of Anglican sentiment, but not all. In the opinion of one Anglican clergyman of practical experience the result of these compromises and inconsistencies has been "a gradual refusal to go to church at all. First uneasy absences, then a longer period of temporary churchmanship, then of no church at all, for people rejected the Church because it was unreal to them and unnecessary." "No people," he continues, "rejects a Church which not only expresses the deepest needs of its life, but also answers its needs" (*We have our orders*, Mculloch).

The assumption, which the Anglican Church has so often made, that compromises, which may be very suited to the English temperament in secular affairs, can equally be used as a basis for the beliefs and practices of religious societies (a view which neither Catholics nor Dissenters have ever accepted) is now being tested in a manner which the Elizabethan founders may never have considered possible. That an Anglican clergyman who must "assent to the Thirty-Nine Articles and the Book of Common Prayer" and swear that he "will use the forms in the said book prescribed and none other", can yet be assured by the fact that Archbishop Usher (1581–1656) said: "We do not suffer any man to reject the Thirty-Nine articles of the Church at his pleasure; yet neither do we look upon them as essential of saving faith—neither do we oblige any man to believe them, but only not to contradict them," shows how the spirit of ambiguity has found a home in the Anglican mind.[1]

But in the world at large it is otherwise; in science and technics, whereby so many people earn their living, exact thought is essential and even in matters political and economic there are signs that increasing numbers (to the alarm of some politicians) are beginning to think. It is idle to expect that alone

[1] "It would be impossible for any intelligent man to give wholehearted assent to every sentence in every article," declares Dr. Garbett. In the eighteenth century, in 1772 and 1778, attempts were made without success to modify the obligation on Dissenters and undergraduates to subscribe to the articles.

in theology man will continue to accept contradictory and inconsistent doctrines. It has been said, sarcastically, that the Church of England has many theologians but no theology, and the future will show whether such a Church without defined principle can live. As Mgr. Knox has said, the English Church once had some order and doctrine; the time of Hooker and Laud; today she has none. Whether the catholically-minded scholastics, Mascall, Farrer and their school, will ultimately provide the Anglican Church with a philosophy, or whether the growing contacts with foreign Protestants at the World Congress of Churches and elsewhere will result in the acceptance of the neo-Protestant outlook of Barth or Brunner, with their contempt of Scholasticism, or whether both schools of thought, though entirely incompatible, will both flourish within the ample tolerance of the Church of England, it is not possible to say. A national church which has survived for so many years without any specific theology or metaphysic may, with increasing bewilderment, continue to do so.

As to one of the Church of England's present major difficulties, its entanglement with the State, a severance from which might mean the end of that Denomination in its present form, the matter in principle has been put with admirable clarity by Margaret Munro. In her book *Seeking for Trouble* she writes, in a passage peculiarly relevant to the Anglican situation:

"Religion, operating only within the State, is bound to be worsted. For it comes into conflict with the most powerful internal forces, notably those that control the economic sources of power, land, or commerce, or credit as the case may be. And as long as religion is simply pitted against these forces it can never win. At best it can register fretful protests which will hardly arouse even a polite pretence of attention. For religion within the State is always tolerated for a definite purpose—that it make the State's point of view, which in practice means the point of view of the powerful classes, morally acceptable to the whole community. And religion will be endowed just enough to bribe it into accepting this role, but not enough to let it become a formidable opponent of the powerful classes.

If religion is ever to make itself effective against the dominant classes, whether agrarian or commercial does not matter, the tension within the State must be counterbalanced by a tension from without. There must be an institution, above the State and out of its control, yet acknowledged by the State, which can equalize the chances of religion at work within the State. The freedom of religion thus requires a moral and spiritual authority placed out of danger of State intimidation, the guardian of the moral and spiritual order expressed in the State's own authority, and adequately endowed that it may fulfil this purpose."

But of far greater ultimate concern than either even the lack of theology or the presence of the State authority is the failure, almost generally admitted, of the Church of England, outside certain very limited circles of Anglo-Catholics and Evangelicals, to raise the great number of nominal members of the Communion from their spiritual torpor. To this end, National Missions, Congresses, Societies and "Movements" of every kind have laboured, with little obvious success. It would appear that the very secular ideal so long set before Anglicans of a "godly and sober life", which is quite compatible with the normal humanism of liberal-minded agnostics, is not enough. The Society of Friends, the Salvation Army (a very different body, but much inspired with "enthusiasm"), and many dissenting congregations in the past have discovered a dynamic (though with increasing difficulty) which is conspicuously lacking in the normal English churchman. The Measures of the National Assembly pour forth in ceaseless spate. Indeed it seems that the principal result of the Life and Liberty Movement, whence the Assembly sprang, has been to entangle the clergy in a net of "black tape"; even the Bishops are not immune. The latest remedy proposed is a new code of canon law, which, however, will carefully abstain from doctrinal definition and so in no way resemble the recent Codex Juris Canonici of Rome. But canonical rules, in any case, are but regulative, and without dogma and sacrament can do little to assist men to reach that supernatural way which is the only road whereby Christians may hope finally to approach to the Beatific Vision.

CHAPTER ONE

THE FIRST CENTURY

PART ONE

THE Church of England, regarded as an ecclesiastical
institution divorced from Catholic Christendom, legally
came into existence in November 1534. It was created by
an Act of Parliament subsequently known as the Act of
Supremacy (26 Henry VIII, c. 1). In its preamble, which is un-
ambiguous, it is recited that "The King's Majesty justly and
rightfully is and ought to be the supreme head of the Church
of England, and so is recognised by the clergy of this realm in
their convocations." This last statement was accurate; in
March of the same fateful year the Lower House of the
Convocation of Canterbury, by 34 votes to 4, one doubtful
—though how be doubtful on such a subject—had declared
that "the Roman Pontiff has no greater jurisdiction bestowed
upon him by God in holy scriptures than any other foreign
Bishop". At York, in May, a similar betrayal of their oaths to
the Pope had been perpetrated by the Bishops of the Northern
Convocation, Tunstall alone protesting. There had followed a
proclamation by the King to the same effect. "This realm of
England" was declared to be an "empire governed by one
supreme king to whom a body politic divided by the names of
spirituality and temporalty ought to bear, next to God, a
humble obedience, he being furnished with power and jurisdiction to render justice to all subjects within his realm in all
causes occurring therein without restraint or provocation to
any foreign princes". The spirituality "now being usually
called the English Church" was declared to have power when
any cause of the law divine or of spiritual learning happened
to come in question, to "declare interpret and show it"; for
which task the spirituality was stated to have been always

reputed and found to be sufficient "without the intermeddling of any exterior person".

The operative part of the Statute of Supremacy goes on to make clear that the power of the monarch is to be spiritual as well as secular. It enacts that:

> "The King our sovereign lord, his heirs and successors, kings of this realm, shall be taken accepted and reputed the only supreme head on earth of the Church of England, called *Anglicana Ecclesia* and shall have power to visit, repress, reform, correct, restrain and amend all such errors, heresies, abuses, offences, contempts, and enormities, whatsoever they be, which by any manner spiritual authority or jurisdiction ought or may be lawfully so reformed, etc.; any usage, foreign authority or other thing to the contrary notwithstanding."

The Submission of the Clergy (1532) earlier embodied in the Act 25 Henry VIII, cap. 19, had already provided that no new canons should be made unless (1) the Convocations are assembled by the King's writ; (2) the King gives his licence for the making of canons; (3) the canons so made have the royal assent, and the existing body of ecclesiastical law be submitted to a committee chosen by the King, for approval or amendment.

However multifarious and confused may be the reasons which wrested a part of Northern Europe from the union of Western Christendom in the early sixteenth century, there can be little doubt that, as regards England, almost the direct cause was the desire of the King for the annulment of his marriage; an act which could only take place as the law then stood with the authority of the Roman See. The legal question, whether the papal dispensation to his wife to marry her deceased husband's brother was canonically valid—depending, it would seem, according to the theologians, on whether she had or had not consummated the first espousal—need not here detain us; it is sufficient to say that, in the earlier stages of the protracted proceedings, the King accepted all the Papal claims without any qualification, nay with zeal. As late as 1527 Henry had addressed the Pontiff as "Our Most Holy Lord, the true and only Vicar of Christ, so that the Head being taken away and the shepherd of the Lord's flock being stricken, Holy Church should collapse". Yet, within four years from this full admission of the Pope's spiritual sovereignty, the King's "divorce" being yet unsettled, the clergy, on threat of penalty of *Praemunire* for admitting papal legates (an act done on the King's own solicitation), had, in both their Convocations, agreed that Henry was their "especial protector, single and supreme Lord, and, in so far as the law of Christ allows, Supreme Head". How came about this extraordinary reversal of opinion? The answer can only be found in the reluctance of the Pope to grant Henry the annulment of his first marriage, or, for this even had been suggested to the King, the permission to marry again, his first wife still living.

Henry himself in his *Assertion of the Seven Sacraments*[1] had condemned Luther when he declared that the Bishop of Rome is not the Vicar of Christ, and was steadfast in the opinion that the "Pope is the successor of St. Peter, Christ's Vicar, Prince of the Apostles to whom Christ gave the keys of the Church". Indeed, since the end of the Council of Pisa in 1511 and the Bull of 1516, *Pastor Aeternus*, few, save avowed neretics (with the possible exception of the Gallicans), had denied that, by divine ordinance, the Pope possessed supremacy even over General Councils.

The legatine court to try the validity of Catherine's marriage was opened in June 1529, the Queen relying principally on her virginity with Arthur as the answer to the attack on the validity of the dispensation which had allowed her to marry her deceased husband's brother. Then Cromwell came upon the scene; he was a student of Machiavelli and he it was, it appears, who first advised the King to make himself absolute in Church and State. It was suggested that he could, by obtain-

[1] It was charged against Saint Thomas More in 1534 that he had "instigated" the King to write this book.

ing from the clergy a declaration that he was in England head
of the Church, gain a local divorce while yet remaining, in
other than papal matters, a good Catholic. Here then, arising
out of the desired divorce, if we are to believe Pole and others,
is to be found the origin of the Church of England. The
intimidation of the Bishops and clergy and the subsequent
anti-papal and anti-clerical legislation must thus be traced to
Cromwell, subsequently appointed to be Vicegerent to carry
out these and other schemes to make Henry "the greatest king
in Christendom", as the delighted monarch was by him
promised.

All went according to Cromwell's arrangement; the
Commons presented a Supplication and Petition against the
Church, whence followed a further "Submission of the
Clergy" whereby they gave up their age-long and essential
Catholic right to make canons with Papal authority for their
government; in future such rules could only be laid down with
the King's licence. Those already extant were to be examined
by a royal commission, to be composed half of clergy, half of
members of Parliament, and only those so approved to be
validated on royal authority—a unique surrender of Catholic
right and practice—for until that time the Roman canon law
had controlled the moral behaviour of the faithful. There
followed royal proclamations ordering all preachers to declare
from their pulpits the supreme headship of the King, and
statutes removing the till then undisputed appellate powers of
Rome; the abolition of the Papal approval of the appointment
of Bishops, and the substitution of orders of the King to the
Chapters to elect his nominees; the penalty for disobedience
being *Praemunire*—imprisonment for life and forfeiture of
goods; the cesser of payment of annates, the first years episcopal revenue paid to the Pope, and first fruits (restored to the
Anglican Church by Queen Anne); the statutory legal recognition of the extant submission of the clergy (this time without
Fisher's qualification so far as allowed by Christ's law) and,
finally, the definitive Act of Supremacy existing in modified
form, as re-enacted in 1559, to this day. That the cause of this

change of front on the part of Henry and his obsequious
followers was not any desire for doctrinal change or any other
motive than his personal intention to obtain an annulment of
his marriage with Catherine by any means possible is thus
obvious the more the earlier history of the great change is
studied.

The opinions of the Universities abroad, even when
favourable, on the whole had insisted, as has been said, on the
necessity of proof that Arthur, the King's elder brother, had
had marital relations with Catherine, if the dissolution of
marriage were to be canonically lawful and the earlier dispensation be held *ultra vires*. The Papacy not yet deciding, as
early as July 1530, the Archbishop of Canterbury, two Bishops,
and many of the nobles had petitioned the Pope, stating that
"they were all forced to complain of the strange usage of this
King who both by his authority and with his pen had supported the Apostolic See and was now denied justice". They
went on to say that "If the Pope would still refuse [to annul
the marriage] they would conclude that he had abandoned them
and so *seek for other remedies*." It was in November of the same
year that the King was informed, through his representatives
at the Holy See, that the Pope had decided that dispensation
would not be granted until the Queen's case had been heard,
this after consulting the Cardinals, and we are informed by
Burnet that even in September, suspecting such a result, "the
King seeing that the Pope resolved to grant nothing, put forth
a proclamation", subsequently embodied in statute, "against
anyone who purchased anything from Rome or elsewhere
contrary to his royal prerogative".

In March 1533 Cranmer, who had previously canvassed
European University opinion, being probably the only conscientious Protestant among the innovators, was appointed
Archbishop. He swore allegiance in the usual way, publicly,
to the Pope and received his *pallium*, though in secret he made
a declaration that the oath was but a matter of form and not
binding upon his conscience: soon he was called upon to
perform his part of the bargain. On May 23rd he declared at

Dunstable that the marriage between Henry and Catherine was void and that of Anne valid. The Pope, who had insisted on hearing Catherine before deciding the case, quashed the decree, excommunicated Cranmer, Gardiner and two other Bishops, Lee of York and Langland of Lincoln, and threatened to do the same by Henry unless he parted with his new consort. Then and then only did Henry, in December 1533, think to ask the Bishops whether the Pope of Rome was above a General Council and ordered it to be declared from pulpits and otherwise that the Pope had no more authority in England than any other foreign Bishop. Royal Commissioners were sent all over the Kingdom to enforce the new Acts and the oath of submission to the King. In 1535 all ecclesiastical bodies by the edict *Valor Ecclesiasticus* had to return an account of their property. Next year the smaller monasteries were dissolved and their property assigned to the King and in 1539–40 the remaining wealthier ones suffered the same fate.

Meanwhile an intensive propaganda to win the people, educated and simple, from their old faith was skilfully prepared, Bishop Gardiner, in his *De Vera Obedientia*, basing himself upon Marsiglio of Padua, being the foremost to assert that the secular and religious aspects of the nation being one, the King was head of both, though it is only of the Kingdom of England that Henry is spiritual head; *cujus regio illius religio*. It was doubtful if Cranmer, or indeed any Protestant, could honestly have subscribed to a doctrine which made the King into a kind of secular Pope, a regnal and spiritual head, an office unknown in Europe until that time. But none in England dared gainsay Henry, save only, of those still living, the great Cardinal Pole. His views as to the unhistorical nature of the oft-repeated claim that the Pope had "usurped authority" have been abundantly supported in our own time by such non-Catholic historians as F. W. Maitland, Holdsworth and A. F. Pollard, but it is not so much what is historically true but what myths, assertions and compulsions generally can be made acceptable to the many which determine *for the time being* the authority of persons and institutions.

That many statutes had been passed in England, as in other countries, defining and curtailing certain ecclesiastical claims, mostly of a monetary kind, will not be denied. So also in the appointment of Bishops and Abbots, disputes affecting their spiritual and feudal obligations had given rise to disagreements and compromises, but to confuse these inevitable frictions with the complete sixteenth-century breach with the Catholic Church is indefensible. In this connection Patterson, Chaplain to the Anglican Bishop of Exeter, has correctly commented in his *History of the Church of England*,

"there was a theory some little time ago, and backed by the authority of great names, which maintained that the Church of England during the middle ages was, relatively speaking, a national antipapal Church. But this theory in the light of fuller investigation must be altogether discarded, the medieval Church of England was 'Papalissima' . . . the attempts of Parliament by Praemunire or Provisors to limit the papal power were acts, not of the English Church, but of the English State, taken in defiance of the accredited organs of the Church—the spiritual primacy of the Pope as Vicar of Christ was recognised—in addition the Pope had made good various claims of an administrative nature."

This frank Anglican author cites the whole field of ecclesiastical canon law, then very vast, taxation in the case of Peter's pence and other matters, legatine authority and the dependence of the Archbishop for powers on the papal conferment of the *pallium* as instances of continuing papal authority.

"From the time of John, but more definitely from that of Edward III., the Pope's bull was required for the confirmation of a bishop's election, and thus the Roman See had the power—not, it would seem, often exercised—to nullify an election made with the king's consent at home. From the time of Augustine's mission every archbishop of an English province received from the Pope the woollen vestment known as the '*pallium*', which was at first a mere mark of friendly recognition or equality, but which came to be regarded as a necessary symbol of the office, without which nobody could perform metropolitical functions."

In the case of the appointment of Bishops, taken wholly by the Crown on penalty of life imprisonment for disobedient appointers, the Dean and Chapter under the Ecclesiastical Appointments Act 1534, we have to note that until that time approval by the Papacy was required.[1]

Thus in the case of Bishop Waynflete, appointed to the See of Winchester by Pope Nicholas V, to take one instance, Bulls of Provision, "By Apostolic authority provided to the aforesaid See of Winchester in the person of William Waynflete appointing him thereto as its Bishop and Pastor" were issued as a matter of course. So also, when the King, in accordance with the compromise with St. Anselm, took the temporalities but returned them to the Bishop, it is stated that the "Sovereign Pontiff has *appointed* as Bishop and Pastor" (a named person) —there followed a renunciation of every word prejudicial to us and Our Crown and the acknowledgment of receipt of fealty, etc., but the fact of papal appointment is expressly admitted.

Finally, when Archbishop Kilwardby, by permission of Pope Nicholas III, resigned the See of Canterbury in 1278, King Edward I was most anxious that his Chancellor, Robert

---

[1] The Pre-Reformation Bishops swore to be "*faithful and obedient to St. Peter and to my Lord the Pope, and to his canonical successors.*

The rights, honours, privileges, and authority of the Church of Rome, and of Our Lord the Pope, and of his successors, I will be careful to preserve, to promote, to defend, and to increase.

The Roman Papacy, and the prerogatives of St. Peter I will be their helper to keep and to defend against all men."

On the other hand, the Post-Reformation Bishops swore "*to never consent or agree that the Busshope of Rome shall practyse, exercyse, or have any manner of auctoryte, jurysdiction, or power within this realme of England*", and "*to observe, keape, and mayntayne and defend th' oole effects and contents of all and singular acts and statutes made and to be made within this realme in derogation, extirpation, and extinguishment of the Busshope of Rome and his auctorytice*".

Burnel, Bishop of Bath and Wells, should succeed to the Primacy. He had no trouble in having him elected by the Chapter. On 10th July, 1278, the King gave his Royal Assent to the election, and on the same day wrote specially to the Pope to solicit his confirmation.

The Pope did not see fit to accede to the King's petition. He annulled the election, and set aside the candidate. Then, of his own choice, the Holy Father appointed Friar John Pecham, who was then a celebrated lecturer and auditor at Rome, and consecrated him with his own hands.

"From the end of the twelfth century," writes the Church historian Makower, "at latest, down to the Reformation no claim was made that England was in purely ecclesiastical affairs independent of the Pope.

The Statute of Provisors was passed under Edward III. in 1351, and that of Præmunire under Richard II. in 1393, and the Popes of that period seemed to content themselves with the fact that the English Archbishops had loudly protested against the enactments, while the clergy on their part had shown their earnestness by frequently petitioning for their repeal. As a matter of fact, the whole difficulty had been very largely smoothed over by a treaty or 'Concordia'—one of the earliest concordats—made between the King and Gregory XI. at Bruges in 1374, of which the terms were preponderatingly in favour of the Pope, and in which the exercise of his providing power was fully conceded.

Many of the resolutions frequently adduced as instances of such declarations of independence prove what they are not meant to prove, for they confine the independence claimed to temporal or royal rights."—*Constitutional History of the Church of England*.

The difficulty is thus not to cite pre-reformation acknowledgment of the spiritual supremacy of the Holy Father and Church but to discover the contrary. The statement by Bracton "sicut dominus papa in spiritualibus super omnibus habeat ordinarium jurisdictionem" may be mentioned as one more example of the undisputed prevailing view. Even Henry found at first that the clergy would only acknowledge his Headship "only in so far as the law of Christ would allow", but this qualification, as has been said, finds no expression in the statute of his supremacy, nor in an earlier Act of 1533, said to have been passed as a result of a petition of the lower house.

Yet, despite this overwhelming evidence in one direction, Anglican Bishops have quite recently had the temerity to rely, in a report of the Lambeth Conference, upon the phrase "Ecclesia Anglicana" in Magna Carta as an instance of the mediaeval independence of the Church in England. Such a contention is pitifully weak. The Archbishop, Langton, who procured the phrase to be inserted, "Anglicana ecclesia libera sit", is there described as "sanctae Romanae ecclesiae cardinalis"—at other times the Catholic Church in France is called the "Ecclesia Gallicana", and so forth; naming provinces of the undivided Catholic Church—the contention of autonomy is unsupportable.

An alternative claim for the continuity of Henry's new Church has been sought in the so-called "Celtic" one, of itself said to have been accepted by a British prince, Lucius, from missionaries sent from Rome. This early church, differing only from that introduced by Augustine in regard to certain rites affecting tonsure and the dating of Easter, and minor details, was absorbed or subdued after the Council of Whitby by Theodore, the Archbishop of Canterbury, and thereafter England became, without reservation, a part of Catholic Europe, fully in communion with Rome, and in spirituals under her doctrine, to continue so until the time of Henry VIII.[1]

---

[1] At the Synod of Whitby (A.D. 664) the issue was whether the authority of "the decree of the Apostolic See" or of the traditions of the Celtic Church was superior. When the decision went in favour of the former the Celtic bishop of Lindisfarne, Colman, abandoned his bishopric, and with his monks retreated to Ireland. Bishop Chad's consecration by Celtic prelates was disallowed by Archbishop Theodore and Chad submitted to be reordained. The *Penitential* of Theodore declares the invalidity of Celtic orders.

As Mgr. Moyes has written:

"The Church of Wales or the British Church never came as a Church into England. For centuries after the founding of the English Church there was next to no communication between them.

Secondly, the Roman succession of Catholic Orders given to Augustine by the Papal Vicar at Arles never died out in the See of Canterbury. When Augustine died, Lawrence, Mellitus, Justus, Honorius and Deusdedit all had their orders from the same non-British succession. Theodore, who did the main part in the organisation of the English Church, was himself consecrated by the Pope, and imprinted this same succession upon the face of the whole English hierarchy.

Theodore's action with regard to St. Chad is ample proof that it was the Roman succession that was sternly insisted upon, while the British succession was not even suffered to enter into the creation of the early English Episcopate."

The phrase often used by Henry, as at Oxford in 1534, the "usurped power of the Pope", was, needless to say, one never used by his predecessors. It was derived in all probability from Wycliffe and his followers, and had lain dormant as an expression of anti-papal opinion until Henry's breach with the Pope over his unsuccessful demand for the nullification of his marriage with Katherine.

The claim for "continuity" from the ancient Catholic Church, save in the case of Caroline commentators later mentioned, is a comparatively recent one. Histories of the Church of England, often going back to Augustine or earlier, thus subtly suggesting that there has been no breach, were popular after the Oxford Movement; one of the latest is by Dr. Garbett, Archbishop of York. The habit of reviving historic ceremonies out of their spiritual context, Anglican bishops being spoken of as "over the hundredth holders of their sees" or the like, is, it is feared, a device designed to produce the same illusion. Yet what are the facts? Apart from Laud and the Non-Jurors, until the time of Newman (in his Anglican days) and Pusey, little was heard of this continuity; indeed the Protestant Bishops of the eighteenth century would vigorously have denied it. As Hume wrote "Henry changed the national religion", Macaulay in the Essay on *Gladstone on Church and State* scoffed at the doctrine of the apostolical succession, as also did Arnold, who regarded the emphasis on the succession as superstition and heresy. The first Tract of Newman emphasises that all authority is built upon apostolical descent, and the notion was then received for the most part as a disputable novelty, however much it may be taken as a possible (but not essential) Anglican view today.

Jones of Nayland, who taught the doctrine of continuity in the later part of the eighteenth century, was looked upon by the Tractarians as an "unheeded witness in bad times". "We hear not a breath about the apostolic Church," lamented Thomas Sykes, a clergyman about 1820; he is referring to the Church of England as a corporate sacred body, apart from the invisible church of general evangelical teaching.

This want of interest is probably due to the fact that most lay Anglicans and many clergy, even today, accept the opinion of Wingfield Stratford in his *History of British Civilisation* that "the Church of England of which Henry made himself head was cut off from organised Christendom". The confusion as to what was really done may have been caused by the fact that Henry, while repudiating the whole basis and sanction for Catholic belief and practice and demanding all oaths of submission to himself, the King controlling episcopal consecrations, continued to retain most of the Catholic practices, largely by coercive legislation. Relying on his royal power, or possibly finding authority in the Acts of Supremacy, he constituted Thomas Cromwell as his "vice-gerent" in matters ecclesiastical and authorised him to issue "injunctions" to Commissaries addressed to all having spiritual cures, requiring them under penalty to observe the anti-papal laws and preach against the

"Pope's usurped power". In 1536, after negotiations with the German Protestants, appeared the First Articles of Religion known as the Ten Articles, more Protestant than the "six" which followed them (for Cromwell himself would have gone to almost any length in a Protestant direction had he not feared the Catholic feelings of the King); he would have reduced the essential sacraments to three—Baptism, the Eucharist and, curiously, Penance. Something like the doctrine of the Protestant Melanchthon on Justification, with a necessity for good works added, was to be accepted together with the acceptance of the first Four Councils. Prayers for the dead were to continue, though declared not to be effective to deliver souls out of Purgatory. Saints were still to be honoured and their prayers to be sought. This tampering with Catholic doctrine, embodied in a *Bishop's Book*, was published in 1537. It contained the following declaration, namely that

"I do believe that the Church of Rome is not, nor cannot worthily be called, the Catholic Church, but only a particular member thereof, and cannot challenge or vindicate of right, and by the word of God, to be head of this universal Church, or to have any superiority over the other Churches of Christ which be in England, France, Spain, or in any other realm, but that they be all free from any subjection unto the said Church of Rome, or unto the minister or bishop of the same.

And I believe also, that the said Church of Rome, with all the other particular Churches in the world, compacted and united together, do make and constitute but one Catholic Church or body. And that like as our Saviour Christ is one person, and the only head of his mystical body, so this whole Catholic Church, Christ's mystical body, is but one body under this one head Christ."

But after the fall of Cromwell the tendency was arrested and a new series of Articles in 1539, six in number, appearing as the *King's Book*, was issued under Statute in 1543. Therein it was stated that

> "The unity of the church is not conserved by the bishop of Rome's authority or doctrine . . . therefore the church of Rome, being but a several church, challenging that name of catholic above all other, doeth great wrong to all other churches, and doeth only by force and maintenance support an unjust usurpation: for that church hath no more right to that name than the church of France, Spain, England, or Portugal, which be justly called catholic churches, in that they do profess, consent, and agree in one unity of true faith with other catholic churches."

In these Articles, Transubstantiation was expressly re-affirmed, communion in both kinds declared not necessary, and celibacy of the clergy deemed essential—this had the incidental effect of forcing Cranmer to part with his wife. So also Confession and private masses, and the Seven Sacraments were again affirmed as indispensable and prayers for the dead in their full intention reinstituted—it was, as Protestants said, "Popery without the Pope", and as such, it is to be noted, proved precarious and temporary. Though, as Bishop Tunstall of Durham wrote to Cardinal Pole: "You suppose . . . the King's grace to be swerved from the unity of Christ's Church, and that . . . he intendeth to separate his Church of England from the unity of the whole body of Christendom . . . wherein surely both you and all others so thinking of him do err . . . His full purpose and intent is . . . not to separate himself or his realm any wise from the unity of Christ's Catholic Church, but inviolably at all times, to keep and observe the same."

The publication in 1545 of a Litany contained a prayer that "From the tyranny of the Bishop of Rome and his detestable enormities, and from all false doctrine, good Lord deliver us", but how the doctrines still held to be true, developed by the

Catholic Church and the Holy Fathers from the original deposit, were to be maintained by police methods, apart from their tradition and sanction, was one which scarcely troubled Henry and his council. For the moment all that could be done was to imprison or burn those who denied them. Thus, shortly before his death, Anne Askew (1546) and others were burned for *denying* the doctrine of Transubstantiation, and many others for repudiating orthodox doctrine. The King, who prided himself as a theologian, presided at some of these trials, as that of Lambert (1538), in person. In the language of Maitland, he had become "the Pope, the whole Pope and something more than the Pope".

Nevertheless, such was the temper of the times, the Bible, not to be read by women or anyone below the rank of yeoman, was required to be set up in every Parish Church. It was derived from Rogers' and Tyndale's translation (Rogers' version, 1537, combining those of Coverdale and Tyndale), and in the opinion of the church historian, James Gairdner, in his *History of the English Church in the 16th Century*, was a mischievous perversion, intended to advance heretical opinions. Certainly, the use of the words "Elder and congregation" substituted for "priest and church", "grace and charity" as "favour and love", "images" as "idols", "sacraments" as "mysteries" and other dubious translations was tendentious.

Moreover in 1545 a service for morning and evening prayer in English, the history of which is later discussed, was compiled from the old Breviary, hitherto used chiefly by the religious. A commission was appointed to revise the Canon Law, its teaching being forbidden at the Universities, while such Protestants as Latimer, who denied Transubstantiation, and others of influence now managed to avoid the penalties under the Six Articles Act. Generally, towards the end of the reign, there is evidence that the Protestants were regaining their power. The Duke of Norfolk, who was said to have favoured reconciliation with Rome, as did Pole from the papal side, was arrested with his son on a charge of seeking the succession to the throne; the Earl of Surrey being executed

C

and the Duke escaping only through the death of Henry. When Henry died the Protestant, Hertford, uncle of the new King, managed to dominate the Regency Council and to get himself appointed Protector; the Anglo-Catholics, Gardiner and Thirlby, being dismissed the Council and the Conservative Chancellor Wriothesley soon after.

From then on the ecclesiastical policy was entirely in a Protestant direction, the only outstanding question being the pace at which it was safe to travel. Parliament in 1547 repealed the Six Articles Act, thus reducing the dangers of prosecution for heresy, and many foreign Protestants came to England to aid in the work. Bishops no longer were to be appointed under the form of *congé d'élire* but were to hold their offices directly during good behaviour only, under letters patent of the Crown. Bishop Barlow went so far as to declare that the King could make any man a Bishop without consecration. Indeed, during visits of Commissioners appointed by the Council their functions were suspended altogether. Even the Archbishops had to take out a new licence to act.[1]

The Convocation of Canterbury was urged by Cranmer

[1] "In truth, the revolution effected by Henry VIII and Thomas Cromwell, a revolution, according to Dr. Gairdner, 'without a parallel in history', made the King the Head of the Church in England, and Supreme Authority in all matters of Christian faith and morals. This revolution undermined the principles of the Common Law. St. Thomas More protested against the Act of Supremacy: 'Seeing that I see ye are determined to condemn me (God knoweth how) I will now in discharge of my conscience speak my mind plainly and freely touching my Indictment and your Statute withal. And forasmuch as this Indictment is grounded upon an Act of Parliament directly repugnant to the laws of God and His Holy Church, the supreme government of which, or any part whereof, may no temporal prince presume by any law to take upon him . . . it is therefore in law among Christian men insufficient to charge any Christian man.' And for proof thereof, like as amongst divers other reasons and authorities, he declared that this realm, 'being but a member and small part of the Church, might not make a particular law disagreeable with the general law of Christ's Universal Catholic Church, no more than the City of London being but one poor member in respect of the whole realm, might make a law against an Act of Parliament to bind the whole realm'. The Act of Supremacy was against the law of God and Holy Church, against the law of reason, against the law of the land: against the provisions of Magna Carta, that 'the Church in England shall be free and have all its laws in their integrity, and its liberties unimpaired. . . .'"
—RICHARD O'SULLIVAN, K.C.

at the same time "to prosecute the work of the Reformation so that the Church might be discharged of all popish trash not yet thrown out" and all was set for the last attack on Henry's Anglo-Catholicism. Indeed the leaders of that opinion, Gardiner and Bonner, were soon committed to the Tower. The Commissioners who had been appointed temporarily to supersede the Bishops proceeded in six circuits; they took with them copies of new Protestant Homilies, to be read in place of sermons. The Episcopal power conferred by Edwardine Ordinal was merely: "To govern; To instruct and exhort; To convince; To drive away erroneous doctrine; To correct and punish." This in contrast with the Catholic pontifical: "To govern; To interpret; To consecrate; To confirm; To ordain; To offer Mass." Never was the utter humiliation of the Episcopacy more clearly shown; the crown visitors were even to enquire how far the Bishops had obeyed royal orders and so forth. All was prepared for the long postponed Protestant doctrinal revolution.

This of course involved, among other things, a complete reconstruction of the Liturgy—the affirmation of Transubstantiation and communion in one kind must go, if not the whole belief in the Real Presence and the seven Sacraments, but the revisers proceeded warily. First appeared a new order of Communion, chiefly the work of the Protestants Bucer and Melanchthon. It did not condemn if it did not uphold the Swiss Protestant receptionist views of the nature of the Eucharist. There followed a psalter, issued under the King's licence, in which it was expressly stated that people were to receive the sacrament "as a memorial of Christ's death, and not to eat it, thinking or believing it to be there really". Finally, in January 1549, Parliament passed the first Act of Uniformity, providing that after Whitsunday no other form was to be used but that in the new Prayer Book; the book itself was annexed to the Act by way of schedule. There is no reason to believe that it ever had the consent of the Convocations. Though the Council told Bonner it had been set forth "by the learned men of the realm and convocations provincial", no record of such consideration exists and that great authority, Professor Powicke, thinks they were never consulted.

In any case, it was the "introduction of a new religion", as Dix, the Anglican monk, has stated in his famous *Shape of the Liturgy*. There he truly says:

> "With an incredible suddenness, between a Saturday night and a Monday morning at Pentecost, 1549, the English liturgical tradition of nearly a thousand years was almost overturned. Churchmen never recovered from the shock. Measures of compulsion kept the churches reasonably full—but voluntary and, above all, week-day church-going virtually disappeared."

The same learned author points out how the Protestants Ridley, Latimer, Hooper and others, save Cranmer himself, admit and deplore the fact.

We turn then, with this sad admission, to a consideration of the new Book of Common Prayer, considering not only what it said but the state of mind of its authors, for this, if not now, later found full expression. In 1520, it will be recalled, Luther had attacked the whole age-long Catholic conception of the Eucharist, both in regard to sacrifice and its assertion of Transubstantiation. Though he still contended that "the bread and wine are the body and blood of Christ", following the actual words of the Scripture, and differing therein from other of the reformers, it is an error to think, as many have, that thereby he accepted the Real Presence in a Catholic sense. He condemned the Mass in violent terms, denying vehemently that the Catholic Church, through its priests, offers Christ Himself in eucharistic sacrifice or was commanded by the Lord to do so. Nor, in the words of the Council of Trent, did he hold that the Eucharist was the source of all graces; to him it is, notwithstanding his belief that the elements as bread and wine co-existed with the body and blood of the Lord, i.e. a Consubstantiation, a communion of the individual ultimately subjective, for Justification is by Faith alone and the Eucharist is, in his view, always dependent upon its reception.[1] Thus what Luther and Bucer meant was (more or less) that Christ's Body and Blood were worthily received *if* the communicant had faith: A "Real Presence" *existing in that sense* but not an *objective* corporeal presence, whether the receiver believed or not. In truth their doctrine, from a Catholic point of view, is as heretical as that of Zwingli or Calvin. It is significant that in the first Edwardine Prayer Book (1549) for the words "A holy sacrifice, a spotless host", to be found in the Catholic *Sarum Missal*, there is substituted "our sacrifice of praise and thanksgiving", and, following Luther, it is petitioned that the "Body and Blood may be unto us", altered from the *Missal* words "may become". Moreover, when Gardiner, perhaps ill-informed, relying on these and other words, contended with Cranmer from his prison that the new Prayer Book by reference to the "Body and Blood", "the altar" and other matters still recognised the Real Presence in its full sense, Cranmer replied that such an interpretation was "a plain untruth". In any event in the second Prayer Book (1552), as will be shown, the Archbishop took care to avoid any such misconstruction.

So also the omission of any preparation by the Priest before Mass, the removal of the elevation of the Host and other

---

[1] There are four main systems of Eucharistic belief:

I. *Catholic:* Transubstantiation, the change of the *substance* of the bread and wine into the Body and the Blood of Christ, whilst the *accidents* (external appearance and physical properties) remain unaltered. This is a belief in an objective Real Presence.

II. *Lutheran:* This, with fluctuations, amounted to a belief in Consubstantiation, i.e. the co-existence of the substance of the bread and wine and of an infused Real Presence; but this latter depended in some measure on the *faith of the recipient.*

This is a subjective and conditional Real Presence of a far less certain kind.

III. *Zwinglian:* No objective Real Presence at all. The bread and wine consumed in memory of the Last Supper; no question of supernatural change. This is a Real Absence. *It was derided by Luther.* That is why they called the Mass idolatry, as *to them* it was adoration of bread and wine.

IV. *Bucerian:* What was desired in England between 1549 and 1552 was something midway between Luther, who was too near to Roman doctrine, and Zwingli, who was too far from it. The Strasburg school, headed by Martin Bucer, rejected bodily presence but insisted upon the action of the Sacrament being supernatural and not merely the natural effect of a mere commemoration.

ceremonies associated with the solemnity of the rite, all indicate that the way was being prepared by stages to accustom the people to a Protestant communion rather than a papal eucharist. Though some high Anglicans have professed to find in this book a Catholic rite they have failed to realise that at most the doctrine exemplified is but Lutheran; again to quote Dix, speaking of the 1552 book:

> "It does in fact express with great accuracy the doctrine which Cranmer had learned from Ridley; rearranged in their new order they served with remarkably few changes to express the full Zwinglian doctrine—a vindication of Cranmer's claim that this had been their most obvious meaning all along."

Thus, in the end, we arrive at a denial of an objective presence altogether, though the change of emphasis is so cleverly shifted that many were and still are deceived thereby.

There remained, in 1549, the Ordinal, the ordination of Priests and Bishops. This was published in 1550, to be modified slightly in 1552 and annexed to the second Prayer Book. Under this six Bishops were consecrated and many Priests ordained. It contains one most important vital omission, but one which might have been expected. The Catholic operative words "Receive the power to offer sacrifice to God and to celebrate the Mass, both for the living and the dead" are omitted from the rite. As was said by Pope Leo XIII in the *Apostolicae Curae* (1896):

> "The words in the Anglican ordination 'receive the Holy Ghost' do not in the least express definitely the sacred order of priesthood or its grace and power which is chiefly the power of offering the true body and blood of the Lord. From the prayers of the Ordinal has been deliberately removed whatever sets forth the dignity and office of the priesthood in the Catholic rite."[1]

[1] In the Catholic Church, however, the ceremony of the "traditio instrumentorum" is now not considered to be essential.

What Cranmer's actual opinions were at any particular time is not easy to say.[1] In March 1548, in a controversy with the Anglo-Catholics, he did not openly oppose the doctrine of the Real Presence, but later, influenced by Ridley, he admitted that he had written his catechism on Lutheran assumptions but that "he was in error of the real presence", so that at some time he ceased in any sense even to be a Lutheran and inclined to Zwingli or Calvin. At his trial it was said of him that he first had been a Catholic, then a Lutheran and then a Zwinglian, and this seems to have been the case.

With the fall of Somerset, the tendency towards what was afterwards called Puritanism was accentuated. Many foreign Protestants of an anti-Lutheran type, Zwinglians and the like, came to England and were eagerly consulted by Cranmer. Bucer lectured at Oxford, Peter Martyr at Cambridge. Those catholically minded, such as the Warden of New College and the President of Corpus, were deprived, so also were many Bishops of the same inclination, Heath, Voysey and Day, of Worcester, Exeter and Chichester respectively, and Gardiner of Winchester; their places to be filled by Puritans such as Coverdale (Exeter), Ponet (Winchester) and Scory. Bonner had already been removed, having been succeeded by Ridley. The Protestant Hooper, after many protests as to episcopal vestments and the invocation of Saints, consented to go to Gloucester and also took Worcester.

To pay for their elevation the new Bishops had to forfeit many manors, and the appropriation by the Crown of church property went on with ever-increasing rapacity; chantry lands and church plate also suffered confiscation. Old service books were destroyed and altars despoiled; all this time Cranmer and his foreign associates were preparing the new Prayer Book. To that great culmination of the doctrinal revolution we must now come.

We note in the first place that Bucer, the most moderate of the foreign reformers in England, had died in 1551 and

---

[1] Since 1525, writes Fr. Hughes in his *Reformation in England*, "Cranmer had prayed 'earnestly for the overthrow of the Pope's authority'. From his student days he had always been inclined to Protestant doctrine."

that now the active co-operators were Peter Martyr, who was appointed Professor of Divinity at Oxford and Lasco, a Pole. The former taught a receptionist theory of the sacraments and denied that Grace was conferred by Communion. Some modern controversies are recalled when we consider his great objection to reservation, even for the sick, also his hatred of eucharistic vestments. It is a sign of the incompatibility of the opinions of the reformers that he thought it better that a child should die unchristened than that it should be baptised, not by Catholics, but by Lutherans!

Calvin also, from afar, advised Cranmer, both through Lasco, his follower, and also directly by correspondence. Such were the men whom Cranmer consulted when he came to modify the first Prayer Book which had previously been described by Parliament as "agreeable to the word of God and the primitive church". Now they declared that doubts had arisen which would be explained in a further book; when it came to be published in November 1552 the changes were seen to be considerable.

To take the Eucharist first; most of the matters in the first Prayer Book which Gardiner, as we have seen, declared to point in Catholic direction were carefully modified to read in the opposite sense. Thus prayers for the dead were omitted, the prayer that we "be sanctified and to be to us the Body and Blood of Christ" was omitted, the prayer of humble access, as it is now called, was put before the Communion and the words "Eat this in remembrance that Christ died for thee and feed on Him in thy heart by faith with thanksgiving" were inserted in place of the *Missal* words "The body of our Lord Jesus Christ preserve thy body and soul unto everlasting life." The *Agnus Dei* is left out and an express rubric (the black one) declared that kneeling at Communion does not mean that "any adoration is done or any real and essential presence there being of Christ's body and blood". This was added by the Council at the instigation of John Knox, who wished to forbid kneeling altogether.

Other alterations were the abolition of the chrism and robe in baptism and the anointing and reservation for the sick.

As to ecclesiastical garments, the priest was to wear a surplice but no vestments, and a Bishop only a rochet. No chalice was to be given to a priest at his ordination, nor a pastoral staff to a Bishop at consecration. At the morning and evening prayer public exhortation, confession and absolution were to be said; this, in substance, is the effect of the Second Book, and in the Communion the minister to stand at the north side of the Holy Table. It may be added that Convocation and the Church generally were not consulted, Parliament alone being responsible. "The Communion service was transformed with the idea of making it as little like the Mass as possible," comments Patterson in his book on the Church of England.

In May 1552 there appeared also the forty-two Articles of Faith published with royal sanction, though the Council said that they had been agreed by the Bishops in Convocation, an untrue statement. Briefly they deny without qualification the Real Presence in the Communion and oppose the later Canons of the Council of Trent; namely those on justification, good works and predestination. Only two sacraments were retained out of seven, and "Sacrifice of Masses" are called "figments and dangerous impostures"—"It is not by Christ's ordinance that the Eucharist be served, elevated, carried about or worshipped". These articles are not very different from the Thirty-Nine Articles of 1563; both are Calvinistic in doctrine.[1] Already, in 1550, the assent of all candidates to them was required as a condition of a preacher's licence. They originated in 1538 at a conference with Lutheran Princes in 1538, though then only ten in number, the later, Calvinist ones, were afterwards added without much attempt at consistency. Despite the pleading of Newman, Ward and others of the Oxford Movement, they remain almost impossible of reconciliation with a Catholic interpretation of the Prayer Book, which is not surprising if that book was always intended by its authors, as is the case, to be Protestant.

*   *   *   *   *

The temporary restoration of England to the unity of the

---

[1] Article XII was expressly anathematised by the Council of Trent.

Catholic faith under Mary (1553–58) concerns the Church of England chiefly as forming an hiatus between the Calvinistic Protestantism of the Edwardian era and the more compromising Anglican, but no less Protestant, settlement of Elizabeth.

During the greater part of the reign of Queen Mary the Church of England was in abeyance or non-existent[1]—it is a weakness of national religions (as was shown again during the Commonwealth) that, when official recognition is removed, they are without a sanction. When Mary became sovereign she inherited by law all the statutory spiritual powers of her father and brother; she was "Supreme Head of the Church", and she was endowed with all those far-reaching authorities which Parliament or the Council had so freely given to their Sovereign Lord.

Yet, as a devout Catholic, she was from the first anxious to rid herself of such pretensions. Having succeeded in July 1553, in August she had issued a proclamation stating that she could not now "hide that religion, which God and the world know she has professed from her infancy—her highness would much desire and be glad the same were of all her subjects quietly and charitably embraced". She went on to declare that, until further orders were taken, she would not compel her subjects, but irregular and unlicensed preaching and printing would be forbidden. In November of the same year an Act of repeal, by abolishing the nine Acts of Edward VI, restored the position as it was at the death of Henry, so that, unlike her father, she restored Catholic doctrine before she renewed the acceptance of the Catholic Church itself: the old divine service in Catholic form was to be used after December the 20th, until then the reformed might continue.

In August, Ponet, Ridley and Scory, the Protestant Bishops, had been ejected and Bonner released. Gardiner was made Lord Chancellor, and on August 29th Gardiner, Bonner, Day and Tunstall were appointed Commissioners to enquire into

---

[1] Two foreign Protestant Churches were, however, allowed to remain: at Austin Friars for the Germans, Dutch and Flemings, and at St. Antony's, Threadneedle Street, for the French Huguenots.

the episcopacy generally. Hooper was removed from Gloucester and imprisoned, others were deposed, some on the ground of their marriage. Cranmer, who so far had remained at Lambeth, was committed to the Tower in September; Coverdale and Latimer had been deposed and imprisoned.[1]

Parliament met in October, but hesitated for the moment to repeal the anti-papal legislation of Henry VIII. They were also emphatic that the lay owners of church lands should not be disturbed. This latter, understandable obduracy Mary was never able to overcome. In the Canterbury Convocation four Articles were passed reaffirming the sufficiency of Communion in one kind, Transubstantiation, the adoration of Christ in the elements, and the sacrificial nature of the Mass. The Anglo-Catholic system of Henry was thus effectually reinstated. So far the acceptance of the Papacy was not practicable, though without it the desires of Mary could not be fulfilled; even Gardiner was still unsympathetic. Injunctions, issued in March 1554, exonerated the Bishops from the need to take the Oath of Supremacy; no longer should they say that they acted under royal authority. Marriage among priests was forbidden, Catholic ceremonies and Holy Days restored. These it may be noticed were sent by the Queen to the Bishops, for in the absence of the papal jurisdiction the English Church still lacked a final spiritual authority; the more so as Mary refused to act as its Head.

But such an anomalous position was not to last. In the same year, the first of Philip and Mary, all eighteen acts of Henry VIII passed since the Reformation were repealed and it was recited that "the spirituality as well as the temporality have swerved from the obedience of the See apostolic and declined from the unity of Christ's church". The nation was to be received again into the Catholic Church and the laws against the papal supremacy repealed. Parliament moreover asked the King and Queen to express the national repentance to the papal legate, Cardinal Pole. At the same time the Bishops supplicated that ecclesiastical jurisdiction may be restored to

---

[1] Hooper, Ridley and Latimer were all more extreme Protestants than Cranmer; behind them was John Knox, who had been offered the See of Rochester.

the clergy. Later the dispensation sought from Cardinal Pole was given and confirmed by Parliament. So that on November 30th, 1554, England became once more, in the full sense of the word, a Catholic country, in full communion with the Holy See.

Before leaving the consideration of the Catholic Restoration, it is interesting to note some of the contentions raised by the Protestant Bishops at the time of their trials in order to understand the minds of those who were so largely responsible for the Protestant Articles of Religion and the Edwardine Prayer Books. Thus Cranmer, being before the Commission appointed by Pole to enquire into his heresies, having declared that he had sworn never to admit the authority of the Bishop of Rome in England (he had forgotten that at his consecration he had sworn the exact contrary), and that to do so would be "to give himself to the devil", continued to argue that by Scripture the King is chief, and no foreign prince in his own realm is above him. "You attribute the keys to the Pope, the sword to the King. I say the King hath both." Like some modern Erastians, he relied upon the statutes of Provisors and Præmunire to show that the Realm was independent—he admitted the authorship of the articles and his writings on the Eucharist.

Ridley, in his turn, denied that Christ was the Sacrament, but said He was in it as the Holy Ghost was with the water in baptism but was not the water. Latimer was less equivocal. "Bread," he said, "was bread and wine was wine"; there was no change in the Sacrament in nature but only in dignity. It is well known that Cranmer had declared in his submission that he anathematised the heresies of Luther and Zwingli among other matters, but as he subsequently recanted, and renewed his belief in the interpretation of the Eucharist which he had given in his book against Gardiner—that in which he had given up all belief in the Real Presence in the Sacrament—this Zwinglian teaching may be taken as the basis of those Articles of Religion which subsequently were reissued in substantially similar form under Elizabeth, and form the present official belief of the Anglican Church and clergy, however much in fact individuals may depart from them.

CHAPTER TWO

THE FIRST CENTURY

PART TWO

IN the first proclamation of Elizabeth, in place of the title "Supreme Head of the Church" (suggested, as Cardinal Pole had said, by Thomas Cromwell) which had been bestowed on Henry and used by him and Edward (Mary having the legal right to use it but refusing to do so), appeared the ambiguous "*et cetera*". Soon however was passed an Act "restoring the ancient jurisdiction of the Crown over the estate ecclesiastical and spiritual" and a Supremacy oath to be taken "that the Queen's Highness is the only supreme Governor of this realm as well in all spiritual or ecclesiastical things or causes as in temporal". The Supremacy Act, the first of her first Parliament, speaks of the "utter extinguishment and putting away of all usurped and foreign powers and authorities out of the realm" and purports to repeal the Marian Act which, in its turn, had repealed the eighteen Acts of Henry VIII relating to the new Anglican Church. It is to be noted, however, that these acts were not said to have been void in their own time, as were the later Acts passed during the Commonwealth, and therefore the question may well be asked whether in fact the Church set up by Elizabeth was not a new one, for the statutory authority of that of Henry and Edward had gone.

As to Heresy,

"nothing was to be adjudged to be heresy except what had already been so adjudged by the authority of the Canonical Scriptures or of the first four General Councils or of any other General Council (supported by express words of Scripture) and except what should hereafter be adjudged to be heresy 'by the High Court of Parliament of this realm with the assent of the clergy in their Convocations'."

Commissions, to be set up by letters patent to deal with heresy, etc., were however once more permitted, the oath of Supremacy above mentioned revived and expressly required to be taken by all spiritual persons before taking office and, most notably, it was enacted that no order not made in this parliament on matters of religion should be adjudged to be heresy—a complete Erastian church had been revived or created by Parliament. Election of Bishops by *congé d'élire* was renewed. The words of the oath were as follows:

"I do utterly testify and declare in my conscience, that the Queen's Highness is the only supreme governor of this realm and of all other her Highness' dominions and countries, as well in all Spiritual or Ecclesiastical things or causes as temporal; and that no foreign prince, person, prelate, State, or potentate hath or ought to have any jurisdiction, power, superiority, pre-eminence, or authority, Ecclesiastical or Spiritual, within this realm; and therefore I do utterly renounce and forsake all foreign jurisdictions, powers, superiorities, and authorities, and do promise that henceforth I shall bear faith and true allegiance to the Queen's Highness, her heirs and lawful successors, and to my power shall assist and defend all jurisdictions, pre-eminences, privileges, and authorities granted or belonging to the Queen's Highness, her heirs and successors, or united and annexed to the Imperial Crown of this realm."

Next, in the same Parliament, appeared another Act of Uniformity. Edward the Sixth's second Prayer Book was restored with certain alterations and additions, the most important of which was "two sentences added only in the delivery of the sacrament to communicants", to quote the statute, "and none other or otherwise". An obligation to attend church followed, though there was no obligation to take Communion, and a fine imposed for absence without lawful excuse. The Ornaments of the Church were to remain as in the second year of Edward VI (1549) until further order.

These were eucharistic Vestments, the Cross, candlesticks, etc. There was a new Table of Lessons and the reference to the deliverance "from the detestable tyranny of the Bishop of Rome and all his detestable enormities" was removed from the Litany. The whole matter was decided by the Crown in Parliament. At no time was Convocation consulted.

It is said by some that the restoration of the words "the Body of our Lord, etc." and "the Blood of our Lord, etc." was intended to restore the notion of the Real Presence and the eucharistic sacrifice. This view, popular with Anglo-Catholics until recently, cannot be maintained. Speaking of the first Prayer Book of Cranmer from which these words were now reinserted in the Elizabethan, it has been said that "a natural interpretation of the words employed forces us to say that the first Prayer Book teaches the doctrine of the eucharistic sacrifice" (*Book of Common Prayer*, Pullan);[1] but apart from Catholic scholars such as H. Griser, S.J., it was left to the Anglican scholar Dix to show that Luther accepted the Real Presence in no such sense, nor did any substantial body of Anglicans until the later days of the Oxford Movement. The Articles of Religion in 1571[2] expressly deny this interpretation, and the fact that, in spite of this one change, Parliament accepted the elimination of the term "altar", as in the second Book of Edward, and all the other purely Protestant provisions contained therein, show how slender is the claim to Catholicity which depends merely on the restoration of the words "This is My Body" in the Holy Communion. As Dix has irrefutably pointed out in his *Shape of the Liturgy*, these words were accepted by Luther as being in the Gospel, but by him given an entirely personal application, in no way recognising the place of the Church or recognising the, to him, "detestable enormity of the Mass." In fact they were inserted to meet the desires of the Queen herself who had a vague, Lutheran

[1] Ever since Gasquet and Bishop's *Edward VI and the Book of Common Prayer, 1891*, the controversy has gone on, and every aspect of it has been examined with learning and acumen by Catholic scholars.

[2] The 29th article (on the Eucharist) had been omitted, but was restored in 1571.

belief in the Real Presence. To her wish also may be ascribed the elimination of the "Calvinistic black rubric", which act again only substituted Lutheran for Calvinist liturgiology and was restored in a modified form in the time of Charles II. The retention of the words of remembrance in the second Book of Edward VI in the Communion together with the renewed dominical words of institution in the first are suggestive rather of political compromise than Catholic theology. The retention of the legal use of Vestments, personally desired by Elizabeth, is of no significance. In fact from 1559 until the mid-nineteenth century they were rarely or never worn, not even by the pioneers of the Oxford Movement, and their use by the avowedly Lutheran Swedes (despite recent polemics in Parliament at the time of the proposed revision of the 1927–28 Prayer Book) shows how little in themselves they corroborate the alleged catholicity of Elizabeth's settlement—the issue which developed was rather one between the followers of Luther and those of Calvin and his school than one between the Churches of England and Rome—in fine the Anglicans on any impartial view are absolutely justified in regarding the Elizabethan Prayer Book as being as Protestant as its predecessors. This view is further supported by the Elizabethan acceptance of the limitation of the Sacraments to two; the deliberate placing of the Communion service in a subordinate position in the Prayer Book after morning and evening prayer; the consistent elimination of any reference to sacrifice in the ordination service and by many other indications that, in substance, the Zwinglian views of its original compiler, Cranmer, were still held. Anglo-Catholics in fact have gravitated back to many Catholic practices in the last hundred years; but that is no evidence that the Prayer Book of Elizabeth, or that of Charles II which slightly modified it, authorises them to do so.

To say as Patterson does, following High Church tradition, that the Elizabethan settlement was both Catholic and Protestant is to play upon words; it is through and through Protestant. It was also entirely Erastian; soon it was decided in James I's time that even such canon law as was allowed (that not repugnant to the law of the land) was not binding on the laity unless confirmed by Parliament. The Church of England, as Elizabeth refounded it under her pronounced ecclesiastical supremacy, was both Protestant and Erastian and has remained so to this day.

The Zwinglian and Calvinistic influences, which, as we have seen, took possession of the mind of Cranmer in his later years, have found even stronger expression in the Articles, the credal formularies intended to bind and still binding the Anglican clergy. These articles of faith, now reduced to thirty-nine, were reintroduced with few amendments in 1563, and, what is significant, approved by both Convocations. Why so little importance is attached to them by some schools of Anglican thought it is difficult to understand. Unlike the Prayer Book, which is a schedule to an Act of Parliament, they bear the approval of the Church's own spiritual authority, and cannot be said, like the Liturgy, to be a parliamentary creation. They were the result of very careful discussion, being finally settled in 1571. In their final form, they were revised principally by Parker, Archbishop of Canterbury, a moderate Lutheran, Cox of Ely, a Marian exile and supporter of Cranmer's second Prayer Book, Guest of Rochester and Grindal, afterwards Archbishop of Canterbury, a Puritan, who objected even to the Surplice, eventually suspended by Elizabeth for refusing to suppress the Puritan practice of "prophesying". But as the Convocations accepted the Articles of Cranmer it really mattered little who redrew them. The Queen insisted on the subscription of the clergy, and in 1571 Parliament ordered that the Articles should be subscribed by all the parish clergy and all holders of benefices. The Ecclesiastical Commission further required that all who officiated should declare that the Articles contained "true Christian doctrine". Today no more than a general assent is required, but the attempt to belittle the Articles as the standard of Anglican faith is not to be justified. Indeed, in direct credal affirmation, as distinguished from inferences which may be

D

drawn from the Liturgy or use of ceremonial or ornaments, they are decisive.

It remains then to consider their tenor; the conditions under which Cranmer originally framed them have already been described.

The original Articles, it will be recalled, were drafted by a Commission which included such Calvinists and Puritans as Hooper, Coverdale, and Peter Martyr to advise the Archbishop; they were not then confirmed by Convocation. On revision the 39th, 40th and 42nd of Edward, which dealt with the Resurrection, intermediate state and salvation of all men were omitted, together with a fourth, which condemned Millenarians. The statement that the Church "hath power to decree rites and ceremonies and hath authority in controversies of faith" was also significantly rejected; it certainly would not have been consistent with the action of Parliament in 1927 and 1928.

The records of the Convocations which settled the Articles were destroyed by fire in 1666, but it seems that they were finally settled in 1571 in English and Latin and that by statute the clergy in the same year were compelled to subscribe "such of them as concern the confession of the true Christian faith and the doctrine of the sacraments". According to an Act of Charles I in 1628 (after they were resettled by the canons of 1604, which left them in their present state), they were to be understood "in their literal and grammatical sense". These ratifications seem to invalidate the argument of Newman, in his Tract No. 90, that they were to be construed on the assumption that at the time of their preparation the decrees of the Council of Trent had not yet been issued in their final form. Indeed the condemnation by the Council of Trent of Anglican, Lutheran, Calvinist and other doctrines as heretical was completed in 1563, having been in formulation since April 1561, and confirmed by the Pope in 1564.

As to the Articles themselves—the 1st, 2nd, 25th and 31st are derived, sometimes literally, from the Council of Augsburg of 1530, drawn up as a statement of the matters on which

Protestants differ from Catholic doctrine. The Sacraments are limited to Baptism and the Supper of the Lord in Article 25, which goes on that those commonly taken as sacraments, naming the other Catholic five, "are not to be counted for sacraments of the gospel, being such as have grown partly of the corrupt following of the apostles, partly of states of life allowed in the scriptures; but yet have not the like nature of sacraments—for they have not any visible sign or ceremony ordained of God". In Article 31 there is a direct denial of the sacrifice of the Mass in the words, "The offering of Christ once made is that perfect redemption, propitiation, and satisfaction, for all the sins of the whole world, both original and actual—whereof the sacrifices of Masses, in the which it is commonly said that the Priest did offer Christ for the quick and the dead to have remission of pain or guilt, were blasphemous fables, and dangerous deceits."

The 11th, on Justification, said to be Cranmer's own wording, denied that we are accounted righteous before God for our own works or deservings, but only for the merit of our Lord by Faith. We are justified by Faith only, said to be "a most wholesome doctrine". A part of this Article, issued in 1552, was omitted later, but the Protestant doctrine of Salvation by Faith alone still stands, together with an extensive homily on Justification to the same effect. It is, of course, like the other Articles above mentioned, in direct contradiction of Catholic doctrine and wholly Protestant in nature. So also is that on Predestination, of Melanchthon's authorship, which is a doctrine of the election of godly persons "chosen in Christ out of mankind", of which teaching the Council of Trent says it is "against the vain confidence of Heretics"—"It is not to be said that sins are forgiven to anyone who boasts of the certainty of the remission of his sins and rests on that alone—seeing that no one can know with a certainty of faith, which cannot be subject to error, that he has obtained the grace of God" (Session VI, chapter eight).

For all these reasons, derived from authorship, language and history, it is clear that the Articles, the foundations of belief of the Church of England, are entirely Protestant, some Lutheran, some Zwinglian or Calvinist, and that where the Liturgy is ambiguous, which is by no means as often the case as Anglo-Catholics suggest, it should be construed in harmony with the Articles in a Protestant manner. The Homilies and Injunctions issued in Elizabeth's time are consistent only with a similar Protestant view. Indeed the whole policy was one of Protestant comprehension, enforced by State authority.[1]

*   *   *   *   *

Despite much divergent special pleading for one cause or another, once it is recognised as a fact that the Elizabethan Establishment was, and was intended to be, a state-governed Church, deriving its formularies as disclosed in its Articles, and, perhaps to a lesser extent its Liturgy, from Protestant sources, Lutheran or Genevan,[2] it is possible to find an explanation of those movements and vagaries which, without altering its essential nature as fixed in the sixteenth century, have perplexed theologians, lawyers and, most important, the ordinary Anglican laity ever since. Once the norm is found to be Protestant and episcopal—the latter perhaps the only part derived from indisputable Catholic sources—though destroyed from a Catholic point of view by rites maimed in the essential of Sacrifice, it will appear that a constant struggle has raged ever since designed to pull the Anglican establishment out of its Elizabethan orbit, either in a Puritan or Catholic direction. Of the third divergence, the heresies which are sometimes called "Modernist", we shall speak later.

That these three contradictory systems of religious thought can co-exist in one Church which claims for itself the title of "Catholic" as well as "Reformed" (see the Lambeth Conference

[1] As the German historian A. O. Meyer has written, "The vast majority of Catholics were entirely left to themselves without any bond of union with their Church." A large number complied with the law, they were known as "Church Papists" as distinguished from the more heroic "recusants".

[2] Elizabeth's revision of the Prayer Book was made by Grindal, Pilkington, Whitehead, Sandys, Cox, Parker, Bell and May, all of whom were strong Protestants, and the first four of whom were "Marian Refugees".

1948 report), an attitude which no other Church or congregation throughout the world claims for itself, is a fact welcomed by yet another school, the "Eclectic", which regards these inconsistencies as a sign of life and vitality. It is true that writers, such as E. J. Bicknell, have said that the Thirty-nine Articles are not bound up with the very existence of the Anglican Church; all that is asked is that they shall not be contradicted (*Theological Introduction to the 39 Articles* (1946)), but the trouble is that in fact they do contradict Catholic faith, which makes the introduction to the last Lambeth encyclical difficult to understand, for there the Bishops are bold to call themselves "the Archbishops and Bishops of the Holy Catholic Church". Indeed the eclectic answer that belief in dogmas which the Apostles or (very) early Fathers had not laid down before the Fifth General Council, depend upon our personal choice, is of course to deny that such beliefs belong to a teaching, much less to a Catholic, Church.

There is yet another opinion, that which treats the Church as a theological department of the State, a view which probably was the essence of the Elizabethan establishment, today finding expression in national ceremonial services, mayoral and judicial attendances at Cathedrals and the like; a conception of ecclesiastical functions powerful, one would think, in the nineteenth century and finding its last stalwarts in such statesmen as Lord John Russell, Sir William Harcourt and Sir William Joynson-Hicks. In our time it is perhaps almost defunct, but students of Anglican history may feel that of all the many theological approaches to be found in the confused Anglican Church, this national one is probably nearest to the genuine intentions of the founders of that extraordinarily diverse institution.

Thus, on analysis, we have found no less than five schools of thought within the Church of England: the Evangelical, the Anglo-Catholic, the Modernist, the Eclectic and the Erastian. The interaction and conflict of these make up the history of the Church of England after its final settlement in Elizabethan times, for, as had been said very truthfully, "The Church of

England has had many theologians but no theology"—
"imprecision" is its principal note and character.

* * * * *

It is the peril of reformers that once they have aroused
sufficient energy in people to accept their proposed changes,
they discover that the zeal which they have engendered cannot
be restrained within the limits which the original agitators
have prescribed. This undesired result soon showed itself,
despite the anxiety of Elizabeth and her advisers to "keep the
mean between two extremes", as the Preface to the present
book of Common Prayer expresses it.[1] As early as 1566 we find
that Parker, in his *Advertisements*, directed that in Cathedrals
and collegiate churches Copes should be worn at the celebration of Holy Communion, an extraordinary substitution for
the Chasuble at that service, and Surplices at other services and
in parish churches. It will be remembered how Hooper had
objected to the use of the Surplice and how Puritans generally
regarded it with loathing. Long after, in the case of *Ridsdale v.
Clifton* in the Privy Council, this direction was held to be the
taking of "another order" to that provision of the first act of
Uniformity which provided that the ornaments authorized by
the Prayer Book of 1552 (which authorised Vestments) should
continue until the taking of such "further order". As has
already been suggested, the use of the Chasuble or Cope have
by themselves no essential Catholic significance; it was only
intended as a half-way house, for temporary use to mitigate
the shock of abolishing the Mass. Had they any tendency to

[1] English Protestantism rapidly ceased to be Lutheran after the death of
Henry VIII. The Continental reformers brought here by Cranmer as soon as
Edward VI's reign began were almost all extremists and Calvinists. They
disseminated their views with much success, especially among lower and middle
classes, the upper classes remaining Erastian and opportunist. When Mary's
accession altered things, the leaders of the extremists fled abroad to Basle,
Strasbourg and other centres of Protestantism. They came back, more rabid
than ever, on the accession of Elizabeth, and it was *they who set the pace* and
really determined the character of the Elizabethan Establishment. Elizabeth herself never got the doctrinal tone she wanted and had a task to control the
fanatics who began to make trouble as early as 1565.

emphasize the sacrificial nature of the Eucharist it is very unlikely that they would have found a place in Edward's First Prayer Book; the *Advertisements* of Parker were embodied in the canons of 1604 and therefore became binding on the clergy. Negatively, however, the denial of the Chasuble and insistence on the Surplice at Communion in parish churches exemplified a practice which continued until the "Ritualist" movement. Pusey wore a black Stole over his Surplice. His curate was censured for having a cross upon it! Not until 1850 did Neale, an early ceremonialist, wear a Chasuble, though in a few places there had been earlier use of the vestment. In *Westerton v. Liddell*, the Privy Council declared Vestments as used at the time of Edward's first Prayer Book to be lawful. This decision would appear to be inconsistent with Ridsdale's case, but the whole matter is really of greater moment to the lawyer than to the theologian.

Towards the latter period of Elizabeth's reign a pronounced Puritanism, which had been implicit from the outset, increased in strength. It has been said that Pope Pius IV would even have discussed allowing the Prayer Book with Catholic modification, but this seems to rely on what is now an exploded story. It originated in a statement made in a letter to Cecil by the English ambassador in Paris. This was abandoned long ago by reason of improbability and absence of confirmation. It was revived by the discovery of a note in the margin of a letter from Walsingham to Burleigh, June 21st, 1571.[1]

---

[1] The note is in the hand of one of Burleigh's secretaries: "An offer made by the Cardinal of Lorraine, as Sir Nicholas Throckmorton showed me."

The reference is to Walsingham's discussions in 1571 about the proposed marriage of Elizabeth to Anjou (after Henri III) and as to whether he could practise his religion in England.

Throckmorton was ambassador 1559–63; thus it becomes a question whether there may have been some conversation (there is no letter) between him and Lorraine in 1561. But this is worth nothing, Lorraine could have known nothing about episcopal consecrations or doctrinal formularies recently made in England, and as a politician he would care nothing. He had no authority to speak for Pope or Council on such a matter, and moreover there was in Paris a nuncio who would have been the bearer of any offer or communication from the Pope on such matter. The anonymous marginal note is therefore worthless.

The feeling that the Prayer Book was not sufficiently Calvinistic grew. John Knox denounced it as popish; Grindal, when he was Bishop of London, wrote to Peter Martyr to ask whether he should wear the Vestments, and most of the other Bishops were corresponding with Calvinist divines. By 1564 most of the Bishops wished to discard even the Surplice, and in Convocation, in 1562, there was only a majority of one in favour of its retention, but the Queen and Council nevertheless ordered the clergy in London to "keep the unity of apparel". Soon an attack on Episcopacy followed, Cambridge being the centre of the movement, Cartwright still the Puritan leader. In London, Bishop Sandys took the same course.

There arose what were called "Prophesyings", under cover of which Puritanism was spread and the Church attacked. Grindal in 1577, now Archbishop, as we have seen, refused to suppress them. Whitgift, his successor, combined Calvinist doctrine with Erastian defence of the royal supremacy and Episcopacy. He did endeavour to suppress the prophesying, but with little success, for the rising Puritanism merely sought other methods of propaganda, such as the notorious Marprelate tracts. Thus the dispute had shifted from the question of Surplices to the far more serious one of Episcopacy itself. Doctrinally, Whitgift was as Calvinist as his opponents; he held the doctrine of Predestination of the elect and the reprobation to death of others and confirmed the Articles of 1595, which, following earlier ones, emphasised this extreme Protestant doctrine. The persecution of the Catholics, the excommunication of Elizabeth by Pope Pius V in 1570, the enmity of Spain and the entry into England of the Jesuits, all tended to increase the popularity of Puritanism. Even the Lutheran doctrine of the Eucharist was being abandoned and a receptionist view of Communion, with the Table in the nave, became very usual, often specially carried in for the Service, particularly in the towns. Indeed the whole notion of a Church, as such, tended to disappear, to be succeeded by a mere personal idiosyncratic view of religion, each being his own interpreter. The only issue between the mass of worshippers had come to be whether they would accept the Episcopacy as a convenient form of church government or reject it; any acceptance of the Bishops as apostolic rulers of the Church was by most denied or forgotten.

The defence of the higher conception of the episcopal office was undertaken by the Dean of Salisbury, Dr. Bridges, in 1587, which produced many rejoinders and finally Hooker, in his *Ecclesiastical Polity* (1594–1597), took up the matter. He made the courageous point that because Catholics had certain doctrines and practices they were not necessarily wrong, and that the Bible must be read with regard to tradition. So that

> "they which measure religion by dislike of the Church of Rome think every man so much the more sound, by how much he can make the corruptions thereof to seem more large. . . . They can say, that in doctrine, in discipline, in prayers, in sacraments, the Church of Rome hath (as it hath indeed) very foul and gross corruptions; the nature whereof notwithstanding, because they have not for the most part exact skill and knowledge to discern, they think that amiss many times which is not; and the salve of reformation they mightily call for, but where they wot full little."

Hooker is a philosopher; he bases his whole case on the law derived from eternal principles; he is in the scholastic tradition. He distinguished natural from supernatural law and insists that authority should be governed by reason. Church and State must be regarded as one, but in the matter of Episcopacy he does not rely so much on any apostolical claim as rather on the need for discipline in the Church, a requirement he also demands in the State. His views later found expression in Arnold and, in his early days, in Gladstone. The royal supremacy he defends on the basis of national unity; indeed the high Churchmen who succeeded him owe much to his learning and exposition. It is of course fundamentally uncatholic since he nowhere recognises the Catholic Church as the source on earth of spiritual wisdom and regulation. His endeavour, also entirely uncatholic, was to prove that the Anglican Church rested upon an implied contract between the Church and its worshippers.

In any study of the Church of England in the later days of Elizabeth the Puritan movement is of importance because, unlike the persecuted Catholics, the Puritans, for the most part, at that time still remained nominally within the established Church, thus exercising considerable influence upon it. According to Camden the Puritans as a concerted force started in the year 1568; at any rate this was the time when they first came into open conflict with authority. Their specific name, as distinguished from that of Calvinists and other Protestants, is not much earlier. The Queen however was entirely hostile to a cause which would take the Church, in however slight degree, out of her hands. As Bishop Jewell wrote to his friend the Calvinist Bullinger, "The Queen is unable to endure the least alteration in matters of religion."

The statutory "Court of High Commission", set up under the Act of Supremacy in 1559 to exercise the royal rule in spiritual matters, summoned the London Puritan clergy to appear before the Archbishop, the Bishop of London and others and proceeded to depose many ministers who objected to the Surplice, the sign of the cross, kneeling, and the use of the ring in marriage and sequestered their livings. A cleavage arose between those who remained within the Church under protest and those who secretly set up nonconforming conventicles. These latter considered that Bishops were otiose, were but presbyters; and, more serious for the State, denied the spiritual supremacy of the Crown; the first since Henry VIII except the Catholics to do so. Illogically they confused Papists with state episcopal Erastians, condemning both. To defeat them, by the Conventicle Act of 1593 it was made a crime to attend their assemblies. The Archbishop of Canterbury, Whitgift, endeavoured to force anyone accused of Nonconformity to clear himself on oath before the High Commission and demanded the subscription of the clergy to the thirty-nine

Articles, though he himself had compiled a Calvinist Code—the "Lambeth Articles"—which Puritans would have been ready to accept, but the Council, and later Parliament, alarmed at the episcopal pretensions, sided to some extent with the Puritans, and Whitgift was forced to conciliate them by withdrawing in part the subscription test of the Articles.[1] Indeed, in Parliament, already there were members who sought to destroy the whole Anglican settlement and introduce Presbyterianism, but were heavily censured by the Queen and Council for so doing, some even being imprisoned. The Church courts were attacked and in the result new canons sought to be introduced. So matters stood at the time of the death of the Queen—the issue undecided.

With the turn of the century, a change is seen to be coming in the ecclesiastical conflict. So far many of the supporters of the Crown's supremacy, such as Whitgift, were Calvinist in doctrine, but now a new spirit, away from Puritanism, is to be detected in the desire to recapture some of the lost Catholic traditions, while at the same time refusing as strongly as ever to admit the headship of the Pope. This tendency, supported principally by clergy, came to be known as Arminianism, named from the opponent of Calvinism in Holland, the defender of free will, Arminius.[2]

The King himself, both for political and religious reasons, favoured a movement which emphasised the importance of Episcopacy. "No Bishop, no King" is one of his most famous sayings. Both depended upon succession, and when Bancroft was appointed Archbishop of Canterbury in 1604, after a debate between supporters of the Church and the Puritans had taken place at Hampton Court, it was generally reckoned that the Crown would support what would now be called high Anglican claims. Thus the Puritan desire for the rejection of the

[1] With the personal decisions of Elizabeth's, the Royal Supremacy exercised by the Court of High Commission and the steady opposition of the Common Law judges, the Bishops were in an ignominious position.

[2] It was at this time that the Anglicans first sought intercommunion with the Greek Orthodox Church.

Cross in baptism, the abandonment of Surplices and many
other demands, embodied in their Lambeth Articles, a col-
lection of Calvinist beliefs never accepted by Convocation,
were rejected. The authorised version of the Bible was the
sole result of the discussions; it was by common consent
agreed to be undertaken—to be published in 1611. Bancroft,
who held that Episcopacy was a matter of divine appointment,
was directed by the Council to prosecute nonconforming
ministers who would not admit the royal supremacy, the
thirty-nine Articles and the Prayer Book; some were deprived,
though Parliament, increasingly, in large measure favoured
Calvinism in its extreme form.

From now on we find that the Arminians, opponents of
Predestinarianism, are the principal supporters of royal
supremacy while the Calvinists began to forsake the Church of
England. The city merchants and the town dwellers generally
were on their side, while the gentry and their dependants were,
for the most part, inclining, if not to Anglo-Catholicism, at any
rate towards a ceremonial view of religion; a new Anglicanism
distinguishable alike from Catholicism and the Puritans.
Denominational adherence became largely a question of
social status, and so remained until all belief was diluted by
Modernists into what one clergyman has called a "wistful
agnosticism": a universal scepticism or indifference, Sab-
batarianism, which later so influenced the British Sunday as
part of the Puritan creed was shared by many Anglicans;
indeed a member of Parliament was expelled in 1621 for
declaring that the Sabbath was but the old Jewish Satur-
day and not Sunday, as was generally taken to be the
case.

Calvinism was also very strong at the Universities. Bancroft's successor as Archbishop, Abbot, was a Calvinist, nor
could it be said that, although the new canons of 1604 made it
impossible for a person who rejected the Liturgy and Articles
to remain in the Church, they were not both susceptible of a
Calvinist interpretation. The Anglican party moreover asserted
a divine right: Bancroft was insistent on the episcopal one, and

Andrews, Bishop of Ely (1609–19), emphasised the appeal to an ancient undivided Church which was later to become so popular with high churchmen until closer historical investigation robbed it of much of its validity, but perhaps the greatest importance of Andrews' writing was the influence which he was able to exercise upon Laud, who, from the outset of his career at Oxford, had been called a half-papist. In 1621 Laud became a Bishop and in 1633 Archbishop of Canterbury.

The preferment of Laud, and his promotion by Charles, to be Archbishop go to show how the Court (unlike Parliament) was tending in a high Anglican direction. The Queen was a Catholic, and it was notorious that many Anglican courtiers attended Mass in her chapel, albeit secretly. The treatment of Montague, who had been censured by a Puritan House of Commons for asserting his belief in the Real Presence and Confession, who had even claimed that the Invocation of the Saints was not improper and that the Catholic Church had not erred in fundamentals—it was said he was working for a reunion with Rome—to be Bishop of Chichester was indicative of the royal sympathy. Laud, it is said, naming clergy as Orthodox or Puritan, guided Charles in his clerical selections; the days of Calvinist Bishops were over.

But Laud, essentially, was of the same school as the high church divines who had accepted the dominion of Henry VIII. He never faltered in his belief in the divine right of the Crown to govern the Church, using even the secular Star Chamber for this purpose; the later accusation that he was secretly a Catholic was entirely false. He would support Catholic manuals of prayer in English, such as those of Cosin, but never would admit in matters ecclesiastical a higher supremacy than that of the King.

Parliament replied by declaring that anyone who "shall bring innovation in religion, or by favour seek to extend Popery or Arminianism, or other opinions disagreeing from the true and orthodox church (i.e. Calvinist) shall be reputed a capital enemy to this Kingdom and the Commonwealth."

This was in 1629—it was the last Parliament for eleven years.

The prevailing notion which inspired the Arminian and anti-Calvinist divines, an idea which culminated in the episcopal government of Laud, depended upon the entirely erroneous notion that the Church of England, as by law established, was in some sense "primitive". In fact, as Dix so clearly points out, the whole notion of the royal supremacy on which the Church was built, which Laud supported, as did nearly all the contemporary "high" churchmen, was, when advanced by Henry VIII, an "entirely novel theory". Not even Constantine, Justinian or Charles the Great had demanded as much. As for the claim that now the King or the Council (or Parliament) could declare what is "true religion" and what is Heresy, such a practice, whatever its merits, can scarcely be called "primitive". The earlier method, which persisted both in East and West until the Reformation, was for the Church to decide what was sound doctrine and not for the secular State. In the time of which we speak, it was the King who ordered what changes should be made in the Prayer Book or worship, and his command, after consultation with some Bishops and Councillors, was issued by letters patent like a grant of honour. When Constantine convened the Council of Nicaea, he did not order their decisions, much less promulgate a creed without consulting the Church; but James I did so. As for the Articles, they were of no more primitive origin in their insistence on Predestination of the elect (based on a misconstruction of Augustine) than the school of Geneva.

The Dean of St. Paul's, Dr. Overall, had taught the divine right of Kings and Bishops, denying Bishops to be above Kings, and his book had been adopted by Convocation in 1606, but the King forbade its reprinting, in that it favoured a King *de facto* as well as one *de jure*; a view which he thought dangerous. John Bickeridge, the tutor of Laud, was of the same opinion—all these men thought to justify an Erastian royal church which they called Catholic. Laud, in particular, did not scruple to use the authority of the Courts of High Commission and Star Chamber which derived authority from the Crown, to enforce his theological opinions.[1] The fact that he placed the Communion Table at the east end of churches and introduced much ceremonial which had been lost in no way made his doctrine or practice Catholic, for above all, as appears in his Canons of 1640, confirmed by Convocation, he subordinated the Church to regal power and taught the divine right of Kings. Even his alleged Catholicism and that of his school fell far short of that of Henry VIII, for it remained based at highest on a Lutheran and uncatholic theology.

Thus the Laudian school, in essentials, fell far short of the six articles of Henry VIII, for there is no reason to suppose that Laud or any of his followers, despite their activities in fencing altars and placing the Communion Table at the east end and the like, ever accepted the Catholic doctrine of the Mass, or encouraged non-communicating attendance—in fine they were ceremonialists and not Catholics. By no one is this made more clear than by Cosin, Bishop of Durham, particularly in his *History of Papal Transubstantiation*.

This is very well illustrated by the fact that even when Parliament was not in existence to frustrate them, the anti-Calvinists did nothing to alter the Articles, nor attempted to remove the Zwinglian influence in the second Prayer Book of Edward VI which was still, along with the earlier Lutheran one, embedded in the words of the Anglican Eucharist. Laud was perfectly justified at his trial in continuing to assert his orthodox Protestantism as shown by his preface to the Articles in 1628. At no time did he accept the doctrines which the Council of Trent had been concerned to preserve.

The lasting importance of his action is that, by concentrating on ornaments, furniture and ceremonial rather than doctrine, he gave a signal for that later Ritualism which

---

[1] Already, in the time of Elizabeth, Burleigh had said that the High Commission resembled the Inquisition! It was worse, because it enforced not fixed doctrine but personal opinions. E.g. Whitgift—Calvinism; Bancroft—Divine Right of Kings; Abbot—*anti*-Arminian; Laud—*pro*-Arminian.

developed into Anglo-Catholicism in the nineteenth and twentieth centuries.

Although for over eight years Laud, under the Crown and Council, particularly in the Court of High Commission, was an ecclesiastical despot, nowhere do we find any serious attempt to reassert essential Catholic doctrine. On the contrary, in his controversy with the Jesuit, Fisher, he declares that:

"To the Romanist I shall say this: The errors of the Church of Rome are grown now, many of them, very old; and when errors are grown by age and continuance to strength, they which speak for the truth, though it be far older, are ordinarily challenged for the bringers in of 'new opinions'. And there is no greater absurdity stirring this day in Christendom than that the reformation of an old corrupted Church, will we nill we, must be taken for the building of a new. And were not this so, we should never be troubled with that idle and impertinent question of theirs: 'Where was your Church before Luther?' for it was just there, where theirs is now. One and the same Church still, no doubt of that; one in substance, but not one in condition of state and purity: their part of the same Church remaining in corruption, and our part of the same Church under reformation";

and, at another time, asserts that "if an article bears more senses than one, it is lawful for any man to choose what his judgment directs him to, so that it be a sense according to the analogy of Faith"—an admission of the ambiguity of the Articles, at one time intended to be definitive.

Moreover, his theory of absolute monarchical divine right is entirely inconsistent with Catholic teaching. Laud, in fact, was a Lutheran, who gave a high ceremonial gloss to the beliefs of that reformer. Jewel, in his *Apologia pro ecclesia Anglicana* (1562), Overall, Buckeridge, Lancelot Andrews and Morton were all writers and teachers who prepared the way for the Laudian compromise—that the Church of England, again to quote Laud, "practises the ancient Catholic faith" and "Church government as it hath been in use in all ages and all places where the Church of Christ hath been established both in and since the days of the Apostles". This is undoubtedly anti-presbyterian and refers, presumably, to Church government by Bishops, though it might equally be construed to include supreme government by the Crown; a view Laud held which was certainly not "in use in all ages". In Andrews we find the oft repeated Anglican appeal to a General Council. He writes that:

"For a long while have we been making our appeal to a council, but to a council duly summoned; a council in which business is conducted in the same manner and order as in the first famous four; wherein there is liberty of voting; wherein prejudice is not set in place of judgment; wherein he sits not as judge, who should be treated as defendant; wherein there are no titular or unreal bishops; wherein the number is reduced of those Italian prelates who, by the quantity of their votes, outweigh all the other Bishops of Europe put together."

The statutory declaration that the Articles should be read in their grammatical sense was drawn up by Laud. On the face of them this was to rivet Calvinism on the Church, for many Articles certainly tended in that direction, but this can scarcely have been Laud's intention. Unorthodox lecturers were inhibited, but when he ordered the Communion Tables to be placed "altar wise" and not in the nave, as the rubrics permitted, it was said that it was a popish plot. The Elizabethan Injunctions had ordered that the Holy Table should be so placed, save when the Communion is to be distributed, at which time it shall be placed within the chancel. By the Canons of 1604 the Table might be removed for Communion even into the body of the church. It is very unlikely that Laud contemplated a reversion to the Mass; probably he objected principally to the irreverence which was caused by people leaving

E

their hats and cloaks on the Table.[1] The Privy Council decided in any case that a Bishop might decide where the table was to be, but there is no reason to suppose that Laud by insisting on the east end position wished to emphasise the sacrificial nature of the Communion. He did nothing to encourage non-participating attendance, did not use Vestments, though that would not have been conclusive, nor in the canon of 1640, which supports Laud as to the position of the Communion Table, is there any recognition of Transubstantiation or anything like it. Canon 7, which dealt with "some rites and ceremonies", did nothing to alter the essential Protestant nature of the Church of England.

There remains to be considered the only actual changes made in the constitution of the Church of England since the time of Elizabeth before the Puritan revolution temporarily swept away the whole Anglican Church. These were effected by the canons passed in 1604. It will be recalled that by the Act of Henry VIII for the Submission of the Clergy in 1534 a commission was to be appointed to settle canons. This commission was never appointed, nor a later one contemplated in an Act of 1543, to be found in a draft by Cranmer revised by Parker in 1571 and published under the title *Reformatio Legum*. So matters stood until 1603, by which time those who wished to learn anything of canon law, owing to the prohibition by Henry VIII of lectures in that subject, could only have obtained their degrees in the civil code. Nevertheless, the Jacobean canons, 141 in all, were issued. They were issued under letters patent, without the consent of Parliament, and in the Northern Province even without discussion. In the first and third canon they assert the supreme authority of the Crown over the Church. In the second they contain penalties against those who deny the orthodoxy or apostolicity of the Church of England and require public withdrawal of such error. They affirm the Thirty-Nine Articles to be "pious and orthodox" and also Anglican ceremonies, and require that anyone who after

[1] The only crypto-Catholic Bishop of the time was Goodman of Gloucester.

subscribing to the Articles prevaricates about them may be removed from his ministry. Such matters as were objectionable to Puritans—the wearing of Surplices, the sign of the Cross in Baptism and other Anglican requirements—were to be retained, and the clergy were to affirm that the Prayer Book and the Articles contained nothing contrary to the law of God. Other canons provide that:

"If any man shall affirm . . . that St. Peter himself (who our adversaries would make the world believe, was then the highest bishop) concurring with the apostle St. Paul, when he commanded the Christians in those days to submit themselves unto the king, as unto the superior . . . did leave this doctrine, so jointly taught, to be dispensed with afterward by any pope, his vicar, led by what spirit is easy to be discerned . . . he doth greatly err (IV).

If any man shall affirm, under colour of anything that is in the scriptures, either that our Saviour Christ was not the head of the church from the beginning of it; or that all the particular churches in the world are otherwise to be termed one church, than as He himself is the head of it . . . or that our Saviour Christ hath not appointed under him several ecclesiastical governors, to rule and direct the said particular churches . . . or that he did more appoint any one chief bishop to rule all the particular churches, which should be planted throughout all kingdoms, than he did appoint any one king to rule and govern all the particular kingdoms in the world . . . he doth greatly err (V).

If any man shall affirm . . . that it is not a sound argument, that the bishops of Rome, in taking upon them to be temporal kings, have wholly perverted the institution of Christ in that behalf . . . he doth greatly err (VIII)."[1]

---

[1] As against all this we have the comments of Robert Sanderson, Bishop of Lincoln (1587–1663) that "the difference betwixt her [the Church of England] and the Romish Party, is wholly about those additionals or superstructures, which they of the Roman faith require to be believed and received."

CHAPTER THREE

THE SECOND CENTURY

THE attempt of Charles and Laud to impose the Prayer Book on Scotland, and the subsequent surrender of the King to the Scottish demands to be left undisturbed, led to the summoning of a Parliament which sat for less than a month. After its dissolution Convocation passed the canons of 1640 which among other things enforced the directions of Laud as to the position of the Communion Table, reasserted the supremacy of the Crown, contained a stringent clause about the suppression of Popery, extended the oath taken by the clergy concerning the discipline of the Church of England to doctors, lawyers, schoolmasters and others, demanding generally that they would undertake not to consent to alter the government of the Church by Archbishops, Bishops, Deans, Archdeacons, *etc.*, "as it now stands established", nor yet subject it to the usurpations and superstitions of Rome. As stated by canon six, what was known as the "etcetera" oath added those ambiguous words to the list of ecclesiastical authorities whose government was not to be altered, which gave cause for much criticism and irony.

This oath read as follows:

"An oath enjoined for the preventing of all innovations in doctrine and government.

I, A.B. do swear that I do approve the doctrine, and discipline, or government established in the Church of England, as containing all things necessary to salvation: and that I will not endeavour by myself or any other, directly or indirectly to bring in any popish doctrine, contrary to that which is so established: nor will I ever give my consent to alter the government of this Church by archbishops, bishops, deans, and archdeacons, etc., as it stands now established, and as by right it ought to stand, nor yet ever to subject it to the usurpations and superstitions of the see of Rome."

This Parliament was the last which allowed, even if regretfully, the continuance of the Laudian system.[1] When the next was summoned in November 1640 Laud was impeached, and in March 1641 committed to the Tower. In the same month a petition from 15,000 citizens of London demanded the abolition of Episcopacy, but all that was done at the time was to formulate a bill to exclude them from the House of Lords; it passed the Commons in March 1641 but was rejected by the Lords themselves. As to the new canons, it was objected that Convocation could not sit when Parliament was dissolved, but the Council advised the King to approve them under the Great Seal, which he did. Nevertheless the House of Commons condemned them. They followed up their protest with a measure designed to abolish Episcopacy "root and branch", but again the Lords rejected the bill, as they had done the former, milder, one. The petition which led to these two measures against the Bishops recited that the divine right of Episcopacy is a modern theory and that prelates had accepted "Romish arguments", such as Copes and Surplices, being Popish ceremonial, standing at the *Gloria Patri*, reading of the Gospel, praying towards the East, kneeling at Communion, church ornaments and forms of consecration, observances of Saints days, all of which, and many other matters, were said to be of Romish origin. The Liturgy, it was truly alleged, was for the most part framed out of the Romish Breviary and Pontifical.

This petition is here mentioned as showing the ideas of the majority of the House of Commons; it was to be the policy under which the successful Parliamentarians proceeded.

[1] "Scepticism and indifference were forms of expression which at the time were little regarded. Men of that age were brought up from boyhood with the Authorised Version; the primacy was invested with dignity both by Charles I and his father—the C. of E. was profoundly and tenaciously conservative."— *The Age of Charles I* (Mathew).

In July 1641 the court of High Commission was abolished. On this Wakeman, in his *History of the Church of England*, comments, "so passed out of English law the last remnant of the Supreme Head Act of 1534". This is quite untenable; all that had happened was that the spiritual powers of the Commission had reverted to the Crown; the Crown's authority in law was no more ended than when Henry declined to renew the office of Vicegerent on the death of Cromwell. Next, in February 1642, the Bishops were at last excluded from the Lords by statute, and in January 1643 Episcopacy was formally abolished and the Presbyterian Covenant adopted, to be followed in 1645 by the abolition of the Book of Common Prayer, a Calvinist "directory" being substituted for it. In March the next year Presbyterian church government was set up under Parliament and the doctrines of Calvin officially recognised as those of the new Presbyterian Church; in fact it was only in London that it actually operated at all fully. Later, under Cromwell, a greater degree of toleration was effected by his Instrument of Government (1653), which provided that "outside popery, prelacy and antinomianism" worship might be free to all believers in the Scriptures and the Trinity, in effect to Presbyterians, Baptists or others in their very numerous and increasing sects. To this extent Cromwell displayed a latitude which was indicative of the new spirit of compromise then spreading over Europe.[1]

Before his restoration, Charles II, in a declaration from Breda, had promised that "no man shall be disturbed or called in question for differences of opinion in matters of religion which do not disturb the peace of the kingdom", and Charles further promised "an Act of Parliament conferring that indulgence". On his return, though the Bishops were restored their

[1] As Mathew writes in his *The Age of Charles I*: "There were two wholly distinct sections among those who favoured Presbyterianism. As opposed to the insularity of the Laudian position, there was a widespread sentiment favourable to a Protestant faith which would transcend national boundaries. The same idea is phrased in the Grand Remonstrance in Dec. 1641: 'We desire there may be a general synod—of the most judicious divines from foreign parts, professing the same religion as us.'"

sees and the Liturgy reintroduced, the Presbyterians were sought to be placated by the assurance that in future Bishops should only act with the advice of presbyters chosen in the diocese, that the Anglican insistence upon the Surplice and use of the Cross in Baptism, two cardinal matters of dispute, should not be deemed essential. The Presbyterians, however, were prejudiced by a revolt of Milennarians, who were soon overwhelmed, but their existence enabled the Anglican Clarendon to urge on the King that all sectaries, including the Presbyterians, were potentially dangerous and so, when twelve Bishops and twelve Presbyterians met at the Savoy in conference on April 15th, 1661, the chances of the Presbyterians were but slender. In fact the conference broke down, the Puritans demanded the abandonment of the teaching of baptismal regeneration, the omission of the use of the Sign of the Cross in Baptism and of kneeling at Communion and demanded that Presbyters should be enabled to ordain. Episcopacy, and other matters of Anglican doctrine, they uncompromisingly denounced as sinful.

Despite this abortive attempt at understanding, a joint meeting of Convocations was held to consider what revision in the Prayer Book might be necessary. On December 20th, 1661, the proposals received the consent of the Convocations and were presented to the King. Meanwhile, another Bill of Uniformity, with the intention to make the Prayer Book when revised compulsory on all ministers, was favourably received by both Houses. The new Prayer Book was consequently annexed to the bill as a schedule and the whole received the Royal Assent on May 19th, 1662.[1]

The rubric which had denied the Real Presence in the Communion, dropped by Elizabeth, was reinstated with the words "corporal presence" substituted for "really present". Whether this alteration refers to a change in the substance of

---

[1] During the commonwealth the Laudian divines were preparing to restore a full Anglicanism at the Restoration, their leaders being Sheldon, Morley and Cosin. They converted Clarendon to side against the Presbyterians and so re-establish the Church of England and the Prayer Book.

the Host, as Catholics believe, or is directed against the accidents, is not clear. Judging from later legislation against belief in Transubstantiation, reading the matter in relation to its context, dealing with kneeling and the like, it is certain that no more than a Lutheran view of the Sacrament was intended. This view is strengthened by the fact that no alteration in the Articles, Lutheran or Calvinist, save this amendment of the "Black Rubric", was attempted in 1662.

For the rest, the word "Priest" was inserted in some cases, on no clear principle, whilst "Minister" remained in others; an indication that the recognition of priesthood in a Catholic sense was never intended. This again is shown by the fact that ordination is altered in form only to the extent that a Bishop's ordination mentions his office by name as distinct from that of a Priest. The power to consecrate and offer sacrifice was still omitted. The apostolic nature of the episcopal office is nowhere defined. As for the Church itself, the Mystical Body being both militant, suffering and triumphant, only that "militant on earth" is mentioned, but "thanksgiving", not "prayer, for the departed," was now added. For "Congregation" the word "Church" is substituted and there is express provision that in the Communion "if any remain of that which is consecrated, the priest and such others as he shall call unto him shall immediately after the blessing reverently consume the same". This provision has been interpreted in law as forbidding Reservation in any form or for any purpose; in itself, coupled with the revised rubric on kneeling, it seems to afford strong evidence that the revisers, if not Puritans, were certainly entirely Protestant.

All holders of corporate office were required by the Corporation Act 1661 to receive the "sacrament of the Lord's supper" according to the Church of England before entering into duty, and this requirement, made without any reservation as to belief, penitence, confession or absolution from mortal sin, shows yet another departure, this time a new one, from Catholic principles.

·   ·   ·   ·

It is a defect of many Church histories that they become so concerned with the recital of doctrinal or ceremonial disputes that they fail to see that the contention between the contending schools has changed, and that in reality, under old names, new issues have arisen.

This was certainly the case at the time of the Restoration; the old Calvinist fervour had died down, save among a few enthusiasts, and the disfavour into which all who would not acknowledge Episcopacy had fallen, as shown by Clarendon's legislation, was political rather than religious. Many of the Presbyterians, let it not be forgotten, had very recently been republican, the Independents even regicides, and the conservative forces which now took control of the nation saw very clearly that the cause of Bishops was closely bound up with that of Monarchy; the Church had become not only the servant but one of the guardians of the re-established monarchical state.

Other influences were at work to despiritualise Anglicanism. The growth of the study of Cosmology, of the quantitative study of the Universe, as shown in the inductive theories of Bacon, the mathematical philosophy of Descartes, the more general knowledge of the astronomical discoveries of Copernicus, Galileo and Newton, and the foundation of the Royal Society under regal patronage, the increase of exploration and the study of human anatomy and of living and inorganic matter, all produced problems of belief not only for Anglicans but for the whole Christian world which press upon many to this day. On the whole, it was the educated who were most influenced by this new quantitative and scientific outlook on life, and as they generally were in the upper social classes, and officially Anglican, the new outlook had far more influence upon them than it had with the unsophisticated tradesmen and town dwellers who formed the staple of the dissenting movements. These latter had always based their creed upon the Bible, unaffected by the interpretation of Church scholarship or tradition, and there what we now call "Fundamentalism" had its strongest support.

Perhaps the most cogent proof of the political nature of the government of the Church, and of the decay of belief, is shown by the blasphemous requirement of the Corporation Act: that holders of office should take the Sacrament. It is difficult to enter into the minds of those who were ready to prostitute what to them must at least have been a solemn memorial into a political test. Incidentally it throws much doubt upon the Anglo-Catholic contention that the Real Presence was then recognised by Churchmen, for is it conceivable that if such an august view of the Sacrament had prevailed, a parliament of Anglicans would ever have consented to its profanation? It was said in Parliament at the time of its proposed repeal that some persons had actually been appointed Sheriffs in order to test their orthodoxy!

In August 1662 the new Act of Uniformity came in force, and nearly 2,000 Nonconformists were ejected from their benefices, university lectureships and public offices. Though Sheldon approved of this Act, he is said occasionally to have protected nonconforming clergy. During the last years of Juxon's life Sheldon governed the Church, and on August 11th, 1663, was nominated to succeed. One of his first acts was to make an agreement with Clarendon that the clergy should henceforth cease to tax themselves in Convocation, and should, in consequence, exercise the right to vote for members of the House of Commons.

In the early part of Charles' reign certain Acts were passed which embittered the Puritans. By the Conventicle Acts religious assemblies of more than four persons were made illegal. Informers against breakers of this law were to receive a share of the fines. The Five Mile Act made it penal for any Nonconformist minister to come within five miles of any city or of any place where he had formerly ministered unless he had taken an oath of allegiance to the King and to the Church of England. Archbishop Sheldon called these acts likely to promote "the glory of God, the welfare of the Church and the praise of his Majesty and his government".

Another former cause of acute difference was the

question of the supremacy of the Crown. This had now become the supremacy of Parliament, and the right of the King as supreme governor of the Church and realm to exercise his ecclesiastical powers otherwise than in the appointments of prelates was openly contested. Thus, when, in order to mitigate some of the more extreme clauses of the Act of Uniformity, involving deprivation of many ministers, Charles, in December 1662, published a Declaration of Indulgence in favour of liberty of conscience, it was objected in Parliament that he had no such dispensing power over penal statutes in religion as his ancestors had certainly claimed and exercised. His words were very moderate:

> "that, without invading the freedom of Parliament, they would concur with him in making such act as might enable him to exercise with universal satisfaction that power of dispensing which he conceived to be inherent in him".

Legally at that time he had as good a case as he had in exercising his prerogative of mercy and pardon, so also, although by 13 Charles II in 1661 the King's supremacy was directly reaffirmed, when, in January 1672, the King declared that "our will and pleasure is that the execution of all manner of penal laws ecclesiastical against whatsoever sort of non-conformists or recusants be immediately suspended", the House of Commons again compelled him to surrender. In 1673 Parliament passed the Protestant Test Act (for preventing dangers which may happen from Popish recusants) and required, in addition to the oaths of supremacy and allegiance, a further declaration that all office holders should swear that "I do believe that there is not any transubstantiation in the sacrament of the Lord's Supper or Eucharist, or in the elements of bread and wine, at or after the Consecration thereof by any person whatsoever". This requirement caused the resignation of the Duke of York, who was Lord High Admiral, Lord Clifford, the Lord Treasurer, and many other Catholics from their offices.

James II, who was now himself a Catholic, when he succeeded decided to bring the question of dispensation to the test of law; the matter when impartially considered was by no means clear and the Judges decided in favour of the dispensing power in Hale's case. To quote Hallam, the Protestant historian, "The Kings of England, not immemorially, yet from a very early era, have exercised a prerogative unquestioned by Parliament and recognised by courts of justice, that of granting dispensations from the prohibitions and penalties of particular laws." It was agreed that there were limitations; the King could not dispense with the Common Law, nor with any statute which was forbidding acts *malum in se*, but the penal laws against Catholics and Nonconformists could scarcely be said to come within these exclusions. In Hale's case, where a penalty was imposed on a Catholic soldier for accepting a commission, the King dispensed and, says Hallam, "It is by no means evident that the decision was against law, former precedents seemed rather to furnish its justification." Thus encouraged, the King extended the use of his dispensing power and endeavoured to make it general. In another matter he was less able to rely on precedent.

The Court of High Commission of Elizabeth, as has been mentioned, had been abolished by Act of the Long Parliament and the same Act provided that no new court should be erected with like power, jurisdiction and authority. If therefore, arguably, the new court which James instituted in July 1686 possessed the like characteristics, as it certainly did, it would have been illegal, in the absence of further enabling legislation. On the other hand, in so far as the royal supremacy had been expressly restated by the Caroline Act of Uniformity, and as James, though a Catholic, was still legally supreme governor of the Church of England, it might have been said that, like Elizabeth, his power to exercise his jurisdiction by delegation to a High Commission had again been expressly reconferred. In any case the Court was profoundly unpopular and quite unjustifiably instituted by a King who held that the ecclesiastical *potestas jurisdictionis* was in the Catholic Church and not in the Crown. That was certainly the view of Mary. The Bishop of London was directed to suspend a London Protestant clergyman, and on his refusing he was summoned before the High Commission Court and, in his turn, suspended. There followed a general royal declaration of liberty of conscience in 1687, renewed in April 1688, suspending the execution of all penal laws concerning religion and pardoning generally as if each individual had been named. The oaths of supremacy and allegiance and that against Transubstantiation were also suspended in the case of those holding or to hold offices of trust, thereby freeing both Catholics and Dissenters. James was thanked, among others, by the Benchers of the Middle Temple on the basis "*a deo Rex, a rege Lex*". So also the King suspended the statutes of university colleges, appointing Catholics in some cases to offices.

Thus, in the spring of 1687 the King ordered the Vicechancellor of Cambridge University to be dismissed for refusing to confer the degree of M.A. on a Benedictine monk, though to do so would have been contrary to the statutes. Soon afterwards, when the president of Magdalen College, Oxford, died, James ordered the fellows to appoint Anthony Farmer, a Catholic, to the vacant headship. The Fellows met and elected John Hough, a Protestant, for which act of disobedience they were all turned out of their college.

It was in May 1688 that James II ordered his Declaration of Indulgence, which he had issued in the previous year, to be read from the pulpits. By this Act all penal laws against Nonconformists and Catholics were annulled and liberty of conscience declared. On the Friday preceding the Sunday on which this Act was to be read in the churches, Archbishop Sancroft summoned the clergy to Lambeth. A petition was drawn up expressing the loyalty of the Church to the Crown, but protesting against the order to read a declaration which was against the law. The petition was written in the Archbishop's hand, and signed by himself and Bishops White of Peterborough, Lloyd of St. Asaph, Turner of Ely, Lake of Chichester, Ken of Bath and Wells, and Trelawny of Bristol.

Then followed the trial of the seven Bishops and their acquittal.

On James' abdication, the Declaration of Rights, presented to the Prince of Orange, and the Act of Rights (October 1689), confirmed by the new sovereigns, declared that "The pretended power of suspending laws, by the regal authority, is illegal"; and that the Court of High Commission and similar commissions were also illegal and pernicious. There followed the well-known clause that all persons who shall hold communion with the Church of Rome or shall marry a Papist shall be excluded from the Throne. In its final form there was added to the dispensing power the phrase, "as it has been exercised of late".[1]

If the last "Supreme Governor of the Church of England" was a Catholic, the new King was a Latitudinarian Calvinist. He desired from the outset that an agreement should be made between the Church of England and Protestant Dissenters. To this end a commission was issued to certain Bishops and theologians to prepare a modified Liturgy and canons. The term "priest" was again to be altered to "minister" and a clause inserted in the Creed dealing with the procession of the Holy Ghost in order to facilitate communion with the Greek Church; almost the first official recognition of that body. Presbyterian ministers were to be conditionally reordained, that is, to "take authority to preach in the Church of England". An alternative Communion in which the words "Christ's most blessed body and blood" were to be optionally omitted, as also kneeling at Communion, was recommended. Nothing came of the proposals, but the notion of alternative forms of worship is interesting in that it was revived in the proposed 1927 Prayer Book.

The King's proposal was embodied in a "Comprehension Bill" and laid before Parliament—it also was sent to the Convocations in November 1689, who refused to discuss it. In its place came the Toleration Act, 1689, whereby Protestant

[1] The coronation oath "to maintain the Protestant and Reformed religion" was first taken by William and Mary in 1689.

trinitarian Nonconformists were allowed to practise their faith if their ministers subscribed to those of the Thirty-nine Articles which did not deal with the doctrine and constitution of the Church. Which they were was a nice problem. They also had to take the oath of allegiance and supremacy, but the Test and Corporation Acts still stood. By the former Catholics were excluded from all office, by the latter Nonconformists were excluded from many.

While a real fear of the reintroduction of the Catholic faith into England caused many of the clergy and others, high and low, temporarily to combine against him whom most conceived to be their rightful King by God appointed, not all after his abdication of the realm were prepared to swear allegiance to the new monarchs while James still lived. Those who refused to take the new oaths included some of the most saintly of the clergy: Sancroft, Archbishop of Canterbury, Ken, and six other Bishops among the number, a few dignitaries, and about four hundred beneficed clergy.[1] It will be noted that these Non-Jurors, as they came to be called, though insistent on the Divine Right of Kings, were in no real sense Catholic and most never became so. The highest ideal they possessed was to restore the first (Lutheran) Prayer Book of 1552—those called subsequently the "usagers"—while others, mostly to be reinstated in 1733, were content with the Caroline Liturgy. In politics some became Jacobite, particularly at Oxford, but that they were anything but Protestant in the Anglican sense cannot be asserted.

Thus, apart from the fashionable doctrine of Divine Right (which even in Catholic France had produced a nationalist interference in the affairs of the Church and its Papal allegiance, manifested in Gallicanism), no real change occurred outwardly in Church government; in theory the Sovereigns were still supreme spiritual governors, despite the many constitutional changes effected by the accession of William and Mary and the placing of patronage in the hands of a body of

[1] The six Bishops were: Lloyd (Norwich), Turner (Ely), White (Peterborough), Thomas (Worcester), Lake (Chichester) and Frampton (Gloucester).

Whig Bishops. No alteration was made in the supremacy of the Crown, in patronage or in the ecclesiastical courts, save that, as has been said, for the time being the Whigs, who had set up William, retained almost complete control; the more so in that the King was a foreigner and a Calvinist; a soldier by profession and interest, little concerned with the niceties of theology. A new toleration, not extending to Catholics, arose, a new type of undogmatic, liberal, subchristian Bishops and clergy who looked upon Dissenters with little disfavour, and were content that by occasionally taking the Sacrament to satisfy the law the latter should continue in their Puritan ways. Tillotson, the new Archbishop of Canterbury, was of this school and he would have included Nonconformists within the Established Church. He helped to found the Society for the Propagation of the Gospel and was succeeded by Tenison, an ardent Protestant.

Thus, with a sceptical Episcopacy and a pauperised and often ignorant ministry, the Church of England for a long time ceased to play any real part in the spiritual life of the country. Such religion as existed was to be found among those despised as "Enthusiasts", the Calvinistic remnant of that insurgent force which in the past had overthrown the Laudian system. On the other hand, the revival of Platonism at Cambridge which had been started by Whichcote, and its attempted reconciliation with Christianity, pointed to a revived interest among the intellectual classes in religious philosophy which had been sadly lacking since the abandonment of scholastic studies. Henry Moore defended his Christian faith as "rational throughout" and like some of the mediaevalists sought in philosophy an "exterior fortification about theology". He was a Cartesian and saw in that arid system of thought an "opposition to atheism". He argued rationally for the existence of God on lines not very different from those of St. Anselm; on the idea or the conception of an absolutely perfect being. He spoke of the "three divine hypotheses" of Plotinus, comparing them with the Christian trinity and accepted Plato as to the reality of the innate ideas of Truth, Beauty and Goodness. John Smith, and Culverwell, the latter a Calvinist, wrote to the same effect. It is the latter who declared his purpose "to show the real relation between faith and reason" and draws the conclusion "that there is nothing in the mysteries of the gospel which is contrary to the light of reason".

If this attitude be contrasted with that of the Catholic Schoolmen, the great change which had occurred in matters of the mind is apparent. That Glanville, another of the Cambridge school, attacked Aristotle from this point of view is not material, for so did many of the early Scholastics; the essential difference is that the Scholastics accepted the Catholic faith as ultimate truth and proceeded therefrom to philosophise, taking as their maxim the words of St. Augustine, "Authority should precede reason when we wish to learn", or St. Anselm's "I believe that I may understand." They sought to show that reason was not incompatible with the Faith, whereas the Protestant philosophers, as a whole, were concerned rather to demonstrate that Faith was not inconsistent with the reason, arriving finally at the astonishing conclusion that Christianity was "not mysterious".[1]

Whatever superficially might be the disputations in religion, in reality an autonomous rationality, which sought to stand apart from all dogma, was beginning to assert itself. Once Catholic authority was withdrawn and the notion of a divine Church, protected by the Holy Spirit from error, had been abandoned, no limits could be placed to speculation.[2] The Articles of Religion had averred that General Councils could err, and if they, why not individual theologians? The dispute between Laud and the Puritans was based on the interpretation of texts and the nature of the primitive church, and later, when "enthusiasm", come to be despised, and had yielded to calm thought, without any prepossessions human or divine, a profound scepticism or vague Deism became dominant in the thought of the governing classes, though

[1] The title of Toland's book (1696).
[2] Nevertheless a royal injunction was issued for the "suppression of controversy".

Catholicism, for political reasons, was still to be opposed and persecuted. By an Act of 1700, Catholics were in law prevented from purchasing land or inheriting it and excluded from all professions; they were even to be prevented from educating their children except in their own houses. The Test Act was here strengthened by direct exclusion of Catholics from all public life, and though this statute was not vigorously enforced it indicated, as the Act said in its title, that it was an attempt to "prevent the growth of popery".

Within the Church of England exasperation was growing against the Government and its junta of Whig Bishops. The toleration accorded to Dissenters, and the allowance of "occasional conformity" in the taking of Communion and attendance at Anglican churches, coupled with the issue of royal injunctions controlling Church matters, enraged the lower House of Convocation, where high churchmen still had a majority.[1] Concessions to the Nonconformists were to them most unacceptable; a wit spoke of the toleration of Episcopacy "because they are of the same principles with the Dissenters". In the result, to stifle clerical discontent, Convocation was indefinitely prorogued. They had ceased to grant subsidies in 1665 and in any case, by an Act of Henry VIII, still extant, a licence from the Crown was necessary before any new canons could be published. The Convocation of York did not meet, except formally, from 1698 until 1861; for all this time the Northern Province was without any constitutional form of self-government. In 1701 that of Canterbury did convene, but seeking in 1717 to condemn a sermon of Bishop Hoadly in which he had denied the visible nature of the Church, it was prorogued, not to reassemble until 1852. Thus perished the last attempt before the nineteenth century of the Anglican Church to assert in any way its independence or the control of its own affairs.

Whatever may have been the earlier or later position, few Anglicans would have the temerity to assert that during the

[1] The appointment of fifteen or sixteen Bishops which fell to William III gave him control of the Upper House of Convocation.

eighteenth century their Church was anything but a department, and a very minor department at that, of a sceptical very
select group of aristocrats who governed England on classical
pagan lines, following their early mentors, Aristotle and Cicero,
rather than a new official church. Nevertheless religious
societies had come into existence under William III despite
the opposition of high churchmen, composed of both evangelical Anglicans and Dissenters for such purposes as the
"*Reformation of manners*" and the "*Prevention of profanation of the
Lord's day*". Twenty-nine Peers, seven Judges and six Bishops
had joined these and similar mutual societies. The Whig
Archbishop Tenison encouraged his clergy to join; evidently
the difference between the Church of England and the Nonconformists was no longer considered important; at least by
some. The high church Archbishop of York, on the other
hand, tried to prevent this co-operation; on this, as on more
dogmatic questions, the Anglican Church was at this time
irreconcilably divided. It was however in the reign of Anne
that these divergencies became acute and the terms "High"
and "Low" Church came into general use. It is unlikely,
despite the preponderance of Whig Bishops, that more than a
tenth of the clergy favoured toleration. The paradox that those
who claimed to be Catholic, and who should therefore have
paid most attention to their ordination vow of obedience to
their Bishops, were most intransigent, and took their obligations
to their spiritual leaders most lightly, has escaped the comment
of many historians and theologians. According to Catholic
principles the Bishop, saving his obedience to Rome, alone
exercises apostolic authority in his diocese, the priest is his
vicar, exercising his rights for the most part under faculty, but
this inconvenient fact has never caused the high church or
Anglo-Catholic clergy (save Newman in his Anglican days)
to hesitate to proclaim their own opinions and go their own
way in a most individual Protestant manner when their views
did not accord with those of their Bishop.

When in 1701 Convocation again met, a dispute between
the Houses at once arose. The Lower wished to condemn

Bishop Burnet's book on the thirty-nine Articles, which indeed was almost exactly the contrary in argument to that of Newman's Tract 90, and also censure such latitudinarians as Toland, Clerke and, later, Whiston. The House of Clergy claimed the right for Convocation to censure both popish and Unitarian or dissenting books, and generally displayed an attitude inconsistent with the tolerant attitude of the Upper House. But the real issues on ecclesiastical politics were not in their hands; long before Convocation had ceased to function the control of Church affairs had passed to Parliament and Government. Thus it was in Parliament (1711) that the practice of "occasional conformity" was condemned by a Tory majority. Since the Test Act, making the reception of the Anglican sacrament a necessity of public office, moderate Dissenters had not scrupled to take it. Baxter, the Presbyterian, and others whose doctrines only differed from low churchmen on the question of Episcopacy, took the Anglican sacrament; London had no less than four dissenting Lord Mayors. In 1711 the law was strengthened to read that any person holding office who attended a Nonconformist place of worship could be fined £40 and by the Schism Act of 1714 no one might keep a school or act as a master without promising to conform to the Anglican liturgy, obtaining therefor a licence from the Bishop, nor might he teach any other catechism. This was perhaps the high-water mark of high church intolerance.

The Queen herself was of the high church; she gave up the tenths and first-fruits annexed to the Crown by Henry VIII to form the Queen Anne's Bounty to help poor livings. The prosecution of Dr. Sacheverell for reasserting the Divine Right of Kings, said to be contrary to the Revolution Settlement, found an opposer in the Queen, who herself believed the doctrine and "touched" frequently to cure the "King's evil". The Lower House of Convocation spoke of course to the same effect, a Dr. Binckes being made Dean of Lichfield by the Crown as the reward for his high Tory sentiments. It would however be a profound error—it is one into which many have fallen—to confuse this absolute claim of royal supremacy with the Catholic doctrine which recognises the rights of Kings only so long as they govern with justice and to this extent accords crowned Christian monarchs support in respect of secular affairs. Never has the Catholic Church conceded a monarchical position higher than this; as the Catholic theologian Maritain writes: "The Church has an indirect power over temporal things. . . . The Church, directly or indirectly, as the spiritual is over the temporal, has jurisdiction over all Kings and secular authority. In matters temporal, the Church exercises an indirect, in matters spiritual a direct, power." Such a claim is very different from that of Anglicans, high or low. In the time of Queen Anne the Tories claimed all power for the Crown, the Whigs for the Parliament, but in either case their difference from Catholicism was, and is, complete. Even the Greek Church, though often taunted with being Erastian, does not seek to confer such spiritual authority on monarchs, amounting in the case of the touching for sickness almost to the travesty of a sacrament, as the high church divines were ready to confer upon Queen Anne.

It is further to be noticed that while the use of the Communion increased in Anne's time and fifty new churches in 1714 were authorised to be built, no attempt was made to change either the Liturgy or the Articles in a Catholic direction—it is evident that even such ambitions in that direction as Laud desired were now given up. As to the attitude of the Anglicans to the Catholics, in England at any rate—the position in Ireland was different—Catholic worship in private houses was not interfered with. Despite the recent legislation property was still allowed to descend to heirs and the laws against Catholics were not often enforced. Indeed in 1688 there were already four Catholic Bishops, and, in Anne's reign, three: in London, the Western district and Wales respectively. Evidence of the activity of the Catholics is adduced by the number of complaints from Anglican clergy and others at the turn of the century which reached the Queen and Parliament. In 1711, the irrepressible Lower House of Convocation declared that Catholics "have been very busy making converts"; another indication of the gulf which existed between these high churchmen and the small community of Englishman who adhered to the old faith.

It was during this period, in 1701, that the Society for the Propagation of the Gospel in Foreign Parts was founded. It had for its object the spiritual requirements of Anglicans overseas and the conversion of natives to the Protestant religion. Anglican schools for the education of the poor were also started, and, in 1698, the Society for the Promotion of Christian Knowledge. In all these activities the division between Anglicans and Dissenters, despite the protests of the high churchmen in matters of common belief, became markedly less.

With the return of the Whigs in 1714 began that discouragement of Church activity which was so marked a feature of their fifty years' domination of affairs. The suspicion of Catholics and Jacobites, rekindled by the rising of 1715 to set James II's son on the throne, played into their hands. The rich merchants who financed the Whigs were either low church or Dissenters, and money and its pursuit rapidly became more important than dogma or ritual. Some of the Whig Bishops were Socinian or almost Unitarian. Dr. Hoadly, Bishop of Bangor (1715), as has been said, was denounced by the high church Lower House of Convocation for denying that Christ had delegated His authority to any Church. He defended the rights of Parliament against the supremacy of the Crown and the fact that he never visited his diocese is some evidence of the spiritual importance which he attached to the Episcopacy; he was typical of many.[1] On the other hand, in 1717 Archbishop Wake, following the Non-Jurors, sought an alliance with the Eastern Orthodox Church and also attempted to come to an understanding with the French Catholic Gallicans. Not until 1719 were the discussions abandoned.

Intellectual controversy with Arians, Deists and Sceptics continued vigorously in a small circle, but otherwise there

[1] Later he was translated to Hereford 1721, Sarum 1723, Winton 1734. The Bangor Controversy brought about the closing of Convocation.

was little spiritual activity. The celebration of the Communion was often practically discontinued; in 1748 the Bishop of Oxford suggested in his diocese that a celebration of the Sacrament might be introduced "in the long interval between Whitsuntide and Christmas". In 1800 there were only six communicants at St. Paul's on Easter Sunday.

This decay of belief in religion and the supernatural was not surprising. Locke, in his *Reasonableness of Christianity*, had in fact argued for an acceptable moral standard and defended belief in Christ on that score alone, while Toland, in his *Christianity Not Mysterious*, sought to show that no Christian doctrine can properly be called a mystery. The emphasis on morality rather than on the divinity of Christ or the nature of His Church is to be noted. Toland was denounced, it is true, and his book officially burned, but the growth of Deism, as it came to be called, could not be so easily arrested. Christianity had come to rest on natural rather than supernatural foundations, and the Atonement had become as unintelligible to the ordinary man as Transubstantiation. Another Deist, Tindal, declared "Christianity to be as old as creation". Tindal, who based his belief entirely on the moral appeal of Christianity, and would eliminate the supernatural, nevertheless died a Fellow of All Souls College at Oxford. The fact is that the astronomical discoveries, now more generally known, dethroning the earth from the centre of the universe, the growth of scientific knowledge generally, the passing of philosophy into an empirical and inductive stage, and the new criticisms of Protestant and Catholic dogma alike, all tended to extinguish the older conceptions of miraculous intervention in the operation of natural causes. Even in the defensive *Analogy* of Butler this new influence is apparent.

In earlier days the scientist and mathematicians were still orthodox believers; Newton, it will be remembered, was very religious. Yet even he did not escape the criticism that his writings encouraged atheism, and Hutchinson of Cambridge and others who tried to reconcile scientific natural knowledge with the teachings of the Bible were for that very reason suspected. The study of other religions had little influence as yet, and it was still taught that the acceptance of the chronology that the world was 6000 years old was essential to belief. Biblical criticism also as yet caused little unsettlement.

The main characteristic of the early Georgian epoch towards religion was indifference. As Butler stated in his *Analogy*, "it had come to be taken for granted that Christianity is not so much as a subject for enquiry, but now is at length taken to be fictitious . . . its influence is more and more wearing out of the minds of men". In 1729 the Heads of Colleges at Oxford complained of the spread of Deism among the students and ten years later the Dons at Cambridge were found to be of the same opinion.

Even the doctrine of the Trinity was not immune from attack and Arian and Socinian opinions were found within as well as outside the Anglican Church, albeit the Government not very vigorously ordered the Bishops to suppress them. When Hoadly in terms denied the apostolical nature of Episcopacy and the notion of a divine church, his views were accepted in many quarters with approval. Hare (1731–40), Bishop of Chichester, was of the like opinion, and in all this confusion the action of a comprehensive State Church may be said finally to have been abandoned. Dissent had come to stay, and if the Church of England were to survive some other means of restoration than the orders of the State would have to be devised.

The obligation on so many people to subscribe to the Articles was resented on grounds very different from those of the earlier Catholics and Puritans. For the first time it was now considered that they were objectionable because they unduly fettered the right of free speculation. In 1772 a petition was presented to Parliament by a number of clergy to be relieved from subscription. It was similar symptoms of unrest and doubt which had constrained Butler in 1736 to publish his *Analogy*, in which work, while admitting that Christianity cannot be proved to be true, he declared it to be the most probable of religions. He assumed that natural religion teaches immortality and God's moral sovereignty; this he declared to be revealed by conscience, so also revelation was consistent with natural religion, but taught far more about the nature of man. Nowhere, however, does he come anywhere near the Catholic doctrine of the Fall and the need for redemption and sanctifying Grace; the whole argument depends upon the testimony of personal conscience. At the same time it is fair to say that his reasoning does not support Calvinism either; it is inductive, rational and unmystical, as were most of the apologists of his age.

The arbitrary selection of certain dogmas and doctrines of the Catholic Church, chosen by the Protestants of the sixteenth century while others were condemned according to their whim, and so accepted or rejected in the Church of England by Edward VI and Elizabeth upon the basis of an imaginary unhistorical primitive church, had now brought its Nemesis. Undeterred by statutory formulations, divines both within and outside the establishment abandoned, on the principle of private judgment, such essentials as the Trinity, the Fall of Man, the Atonement, Redemption and the Resurrection. Adherence to the Establishment had in very many cases become but nominal, and, despite many contentious pamphlets, books and polemics, no person was strong enough to cope with the prevailing infidelity and disorder.

The proposal of Anne to build fifty churches in London was quietly dropped, the suggestion of bishoprics in Jamaica, Barbados and other places was abandoned and the physical condition of church buildings at home largely neglected. Many fabrics of mediaeval beauty as had not been despoiled by the Puritans were profaned by coats of whitewash and stucco.[1]

---

[1] Later important ones were built by Gibbs and Hawksmoor. On one, the figure on top of the steeple of St. George's, Bloomsbury, was King George I. Hence the contemporary rhyme:

> When Harry the Eighth left the Pope in the lurch
> The Protestants made him the Head of the Church;
> But George's good subjects, the Bloomsbury people,
> Instead of the Church, made him head of the steeple.

The Communion table was often in decay, covered with some damp rotting cloth. Woodwork was dilapidated and the whole edifice neglected. The services were perfunctory, instruction evaded, Confirmation neglected, and Communion rare. Preaching was confined for the most part to vague moralising and denunciation of the errors of Rome and no new endowments forthcoming. The Bishops, who spent most of their time supporting the Government in the House of Lords, alone showed any sign of prosperity, and they were chosen much more for their political reliability than their devotion to religion. Until 1782 many clergy held their livings from patrons on the condition of resignation when called upon. These "bonds" were then at length declared illegal. There was much writing on Church matters, such as Law's answer to Hoadly, the *Three Letters to the Bishop of Bangor*, who had added to his denial of the corporate nature of the Church an affirmation that the Eucharist was merely commemorative, an attitude quite justifiable under the Zwinglian articles of religion. Law's *Serious Call to a Devout and Holy Life* (1728) is said to have inspired Wesley and inaugurated the Evangelical revival, but until that time the Church of England—to apply Stevenson's description of a railway station on a Sunday—may fairly be said to have been the "temple of a dead religion".[1]

[1] After the Restoration it was said that many incumbents had more to say about King Charles the Martyr than about Jesus Christ. But under the Hanoverians King Charles was not so acceptable a topic, especially when there had been two risings to bring back the Stuarts. Everybody was sick of the disputations of Puritans, Presbyterians, Independents, Quakers, etc., etc. The only topics left were "the errors and usurpations of the Pope of Rome", the Armada and the Gunpowder Plot.

CHAPTER FOUR

THE THIRD CENTURY

THE revival of the Anglican Church, paradoxically, is due in the main to Nonconformity. From 1689, when the Toleration Act was passed, meeting houses, duly licensed, were recognised by law, as were the trusts and property of those who met in them, and by 1720 there were at least four thousand buildings in which Dissenters might assemble.[1] In 1711 the Occasional Conformity Act was repealed, and though the Test Act (chiefly directed against Catholics) and the Corporation Acts remained, they gradually ceased to be enforced and Nonconformist ministers attained to a tolerated status. Many of them rejoined the Church and to that extent reanimated that lethargic body, but again the perils of unrestricted private judgment appeared; divergencies of belief and worship developed, indeed many of the Dissenters were Socinian or Arian in belief, and all dogmatic teaching was unpopular. So we come to Wesley, an ordained minister of the Anglican Church. He had undergone a conversion and, feeling that his sins had been taken away by Christ, he emphasised over and over again the saving power of the Atonement. His appeal was mostly to the lowly. He and George Whitfield, disregarding parochial etiquette, preached all over the country to immense audiences.

The Methodists, with whom his name is so closely associated, was a name given to a number of students at Oxford, the home of so many religious movements, who about 1730 began of purpose to live a religious life. They communicated every week, fasted, did social work and had discussions on biblical subjects. Wesley was their leader. In all they numbered at the outset but fifteen, Charles Wesley and Whitfield among

[1] At this time there were still twenty *Huguenot* churches in London; there had been thirty. There were still eleven in 1782.

them, also Hervey, the author of the then popular *Meditations*. Both he and Whitfield inclined to Calvinism in theology, while John Wesley himself at this time was a Lutheran churchman. His attitude to Dissenters was severe, sometimes refusing them Communion and even the Burial Service. He ministered for a time in Georgia, where he came into contact with the Moravian sect and soon became concerned, on his return to England, with the doctrine of Justification, on which subject the Anglican Church had taken such conflicting opinions. The orthodox belief that Christ was sacrificed in expiation of our sins became to him the essence of salvation, and thereafter, a more debatable opinion, once that conviction was established, a freedom for the individual from sin was achieved. Such a view, familiar to Puritan theology, was, of its nature, inconsistent with the Catholic doctrine of sacramental grace and the necessity for good works, not to mention free will, and is in substance condemned by the Council of Trent. Yet, of itself, it was held, probably by a majority of Anglicans at the time, and, as has been said, was entirely consistent with the Thirty-nine Articles which, in terms, accept the doctrine.

The hostility of the clergy, it must be made clear, was not due to Wesley's Protestant theology; it was the fact that the Methodists accepted the Articles and Homilies with such fervour which disgusted their fellow ministers; their general "enthusiasm" and intransigence. Yet, if judged by the formulae of the Anglican articles, they were more orthodox than were the majority of the clergy. But, as Lecky writes, "The love of order, routine and decorum, which was the strongest feeling in the clerical mind, was violently shocked."

By 1740 most of the prominent Methodists had been excluded from Anglican pulpits, and in consequence began to erect their own chapels. Whitfield (who differed from Wesley in being more Calvinistic) took to preaching in the open air, mostly to miners and artisans, and he persuaded the Wesleys to follow him in this work.

Whitfield was an ordained Anglican and accepted the

Thirty-nine Articles, as why should he not? Unlike Wesley, he cared nothing for ecclesiastical problems and never considered that he might be creating a schism; a danger which worried Wesley very much at one time. Consistently with his general outlook, Whitfield cared little for the Church of England as such; his appeal was personal and unsacramental, resembling rather that of the later Salvation Army.[1]

It was from this activity that the "Evangelicals", those sympathisers with Wesley who remained within the Anglican Church, took their inspiration. Their progress and influence cannot rightly be assessed without considering their Methodist sympathies, as the Methodists, in their turn, had been influenced by that German Protestant sect, the Moravians. This sect, whose earlier history and aberrations need not detain us, by the time they came to England had become a non-sacramental, Calvinist body of enthusiastic missionaries, appealing to Christians to rely solely on the belief in the Atonement and the innate depravity of man. Indeed it is just in this acceptance of man's inherent vileness that we find a common creed among all the variety of Evangelicals. A justification for this view may be found in Articles 10 to 18 of the Church of England.

Confining our attention to those who remained within the Church of England, we find that at first the divergence in the evangelical movement between them and the Dissenters was very slight. Berridge, rector of Everton, continued to hold his cure but went round the country, like Wesley, preaching, entering other incumbents' parishes without their leave and stimulating lay preachers. Other Anglicans of the same kind were Grimshaw, ordained in 1731, Romaine, a great adherent of the doctrine of Justification by Faith alone, Venn of Huddersfield, and, most important, Simeon of Cambridge.

[1] The Wesleyans and Congregationalists, however, were inclined to accept the Catholic notion of the Natural Law. Natural theology to the Lutheran is an obstacle to the acceptance of Grace, and, being human, injurious to complete conversion.

All of these men were bitterly anti-Catholic;[1] they regarded the Church at highest as a mere ecclesiastical convenience and were ignorant, for the most part, of theology. Yet their emotional powers and personal sacrifices gave them great influence; they were compared, to their advantage, with the affluent Erastian Bishops and lethargic country clergymen. From them derived Wilberforce, the emancipator of slaves, and Zachary Macaulay, and their work in education and the treatment of criminals and the unfortunate undoubtedly inspired the subsequent efforts of Lord Shaftesbury and the humanitarian movements of the Victorian era. The foundation of the Church Missionary Society in 1799 and the Bible Society in 1804 was largely their work. On the other hand, they were very ignorant of Church history, their theological knowledge was negligible and they discounted the use of reason, relying principally on emotional satisfaction. So, when the time for resistance to the new scepticism came in the nineteenth century, they proved utterly incapable of contesting it; their objection to enjoyment, based probably on their belief in man's wickedness and a certain Manichean distrust of material things, art, and normal human pleasures, rendered them unpopular to many.

Thus by the end of the eighteenth century the Church of England found itself divided, socially and religiously, into two classes: the conservative, well-connected clergy living quietly in comfortable rural surroundings, often closely related to the Squire, Tory for the most part in politics, interested in sport and rural life, scarcely distinguishable from their social lay equals, often high church in religion; and the new Evangelicals, urban mostly in origin who, like their more complacent fellow clergymen, were ignorant of theology, but made up for that deficiency by zeal and missionary appeal. The Prime Minister, Mr. Perceval, was of their persuasion and the royal

[1] Yet in 1791 and 1793, doubtless as a result of the French Revolution, Catholics were relieved from registering their priests and chapels. In 1828 the Test and Corporation Acts were repealed. In 1812 the Conventicle and Five Mile Acts were also repealed, a privilege extended to Unitarians in 1813.

family in George III's time much attracted: but the aristocracy as a whole stood aloof, sarcastic and sceptical.

Clapham in London, and the University of Cambridge, were centres of the evangelical faith at the turn of the century. Charles Simeon was their leader. Many societies were formed to spread their opinions and incumbents with their views were to be found in parishes throughout the country. Of others of like opinion we may mention Hannah Moore and Robert Raikes, the founder of Sunday Schools.[1]

The influence on the Church of England of all this activity was profound; it lessened the distinction between Evangelicals, Anglicans and Dissenters, discounted whatever belief in a corporate teaching and divinely-inspired Church still existed, discouraged the use of the Sacraments in the interests of a subjective conviction of personal salvation, and—somewhat inconsistently—having regard to its official disbelief in the theological value of good works, in fact actively encouraged them. The Evangelicals for the most part were without intellectual power and of Catholic doctrine knew nothing; indeed it may be said that never was the Church of England so entirely lacking in thought as at this period. The few Anglicans who still believed in the apostolical succession or wished to revive the first Prayer Book of Edward VI or who preached the Real Presence were ignored; indeed the Non-Jurors, which body contained most of them, was by 1780 almost extinct.

The Evangelical movement generally, as Cardinal Newman, who was brought up in it, has pointed out, was derived from the Puritans. The Scriptures, excluding the Church as interpreter of them, was the source of truth, each man interpreting by his own private judgment. The fact that the Church existed before the New Testament was forgotten or ignored; the Gospel had only to be preached and the

[1] The relief from certain disabilities of Catholics concerning inheritance in 1778 led to a Protestant Association under Lord George Gordon organising serious riots. The effect was to induce many Evangelicals to remain within the respectable Anglican Church.

sinner convinced of his salvation and all was achieved. The clergy were deemed to be but ministers and not the stewards of the mysteries of God. All this was consistent with the saying in the Articles that "Holy Scripture contains all things necessary to salvation". At the same time, while emphasising the love of Christ, fear of the wrath of God formed a large part of the Evangelical appeal.

The Evangelical attitude towards Predestinarianism was confused and evasive. "Like most evangelicals of my youth," wrote Newman, "Mayers did not explain away the seventeenth Article on Predestination, but bowed under it with shuddering." Manning, who, although his family was "old-fashioned high church", was himself, at the time of his ordination, inclined to be an Evangelical. As he has said, "I was a pietist until I accepted the Tridentine decrees." The teaching he early received was based entirely on the Bible. "In 1833"—his first year as a curate at Lavington—he says, "I had thought and read myself out of contact with every system known to me. Anglicanism was formal, Evangelicalism illogical and at variance with the New Testament, Nonconformity was to me mere disorder. Of the Catholic Church I knew nothing." If such a thinker as Manning could admit the confusion in which, as an Anglican clergyman, he found himself, what was the position of the ordinary uninstructed cleric or layman?

In truth, by 1830 the old Evangelicalism was failing; its appeal was being directed rather to social than to direct religious ends. It was becoming associated with the new radical reform movement and, forgetting the Calvinistic faith, worked for justice in this world. In politics the Evangelicals were mostly Liberal, but hesitated to associate themselves too closely with the old Whig Erastian ideal of a church directed by the State. Nevertheless, unlike the majority of the Bishops, they supported the new Reform Bill and agreed with Lord John Russell that the "Bishops should set their house in order". The suppression of some Irish bishoprics which led Keble to denounce this "national apostasy" moved them not at all, for to them Episcopacy had no significance; many doubted if the institution had biblical authority at all. The adjustment of the endowments of bishoprics (the average was then £6000 a year) was supported for the most part by the Evangelicals.[1]

Meanwhile a new force, at least one so far not very active, the "Broad Church", was attacking the Evangelicals on their most exposed flank, their lack of intellectual defence. Having no authoritative sanction for belief, any criticism of their interpretation of the Bible could not but be menacing. Oxford in the eighteen-thirties, unlike Cambridge, still required subscription to the Thirty-nine Articles on matriculation and this obligation Dr. Hampden, in 1832, in his Bampton Lecture, wished to abolish. He denied the authority of the teaching Church and so far might have pleased the Evangelicals, but went on, to their dismay, to throw doubt upon the necessity for the acceptance of the Nicene, Athanasian or other creeds except for purposes of "denying error". Primitive faith, he contended, did not require them. All this was as alarming to the Evangelical as to the new Tractarian schools and by their joint effort he was deprived of his right, as Regius Professor of Divinity, to nominate select preachers for the University.

Despite the attack upon the Latitudinarians, or "Liberals", as Newman calls them, by the Evangelicals and the now rising Anglo-Catholic schools of thought, it would be an error to confuse the Latitudinarians with later Modernists. Arnold, one of their leaders, was a devout believer in the divinity of Christ and indeed in the reliability of the whole of the Bible. He and his followers wished to see the State coterminus with the invisible Church of all Christians, into which he would admit Dissenters of all kinds of opinion; even, perhaps, Unitarians.

[1] The record of the Anglican episcopacy in the early nineteenth century was consistently illiberal. In 1833, the Archbishop of Canterbury opposed a Bill to remove Jewish disabilities; in 1858, the Bishops and Dr. Arnold were still opposing; in 1865, ten Bishops opposed a Bill to allow Nonconformists to take public office; in 1854, Dissenters were reluctantly allowed to be students, but a man could not take a degree unless prepared to accept the Thirty-nine Articles; not till 1876 were tests abolished; not until 1868 were Church rates abolished; as late as 1860, sixteen Bishops had voted against abolition.

He denied the Catholic belief in the operation of Grace through the Sacraments and equally the Evangelical idea of Grace falling on the elect; a moral life in his view best proved Christian belief. As to supernatural assumptions he was indifferent, being spiritually pragmatical and interested only in Christian behaviour as such.[1]

This denial of any principle in the Church made it increasingly difficult, when biblical criticism, scientific discovery and comparative religious study began to exercise influence, for the Liberals to resist a trend towards Modernism and eventually towards complete Scepticism; but this was later to come. For the moment Hampden, Arnold, Stanley and their liberal school (to quote Dean Church), "though without much devotional temper, were penetrated by a sense of the reality and seriousness of religion".

Finally, there is to be noted, perhaps most important of all for the future, the growth, particularly in Oxford during this challenging time of the Anglican Church, of an organised effort to recapture the long-lost belief in the Church as the mystical body of Christ, its apostolicity and its sacramental system; that movement which has come to be known as Tractarian. Its origins are perhaps to be found in that Laudian and Non-Juring movement, but there was one great difference which has so far almost escaped notice: the disciples of Laud accepted without qualification the principle of the Divine Right of Kings and were in no sense perturbed that the Crown should be acclaimed Supreme Governor of the Church, albeit the King did not claim to exercise sacerdotal functions. With the Tractarians the relation of Crown and Church was never fairly met; they appear to have been ignorant of the distinction made by St. Thomas Aquinas and other Catholic thinkers between the direct and the indirect power of the Church and the right of Sovereigns to rule in the secular field so long as

[1] In practice the Protestant does not really interpret the Bible for himself. but, having got rid of the great theologians, the specialists, takes his interpretation from some lay preacher or his mother or the "great Protestant tradition". —MAISIE WARD in *The Wilfrid Wards*.

they acted in accordance with natural justice. Consequently, when in 1833 Keble preached his famous assize sermon and denounced the Government, describing its suppression of some Irish Anglican dioceses as "a direct disavowal of the government of God", and spoke of "the apostolic Church in these realms", he did not face the fact that the Crown was acting with the advice of its ministers and the consent of Parliament, and he did not even suggest disestablishment, a course which would have been abhorrent to his Tory principles. So also—when another pioneer of the Tractarian cause wrote that "our prelates are insulted by Ministers of State"—he did not question the right of the Crown, through the nominal process of the *congé d'élire*, to appoint them. The constitutional problem which had so exercised the minds of churchmen and laity during the earlier centuries was ignored.

The vital question Newman wrote in the *Apologia* was, "How were we to keep the Church from being liberalised?" The Bishop of London had declared that the belief in the apostolical succession had gone out with the Non-Jurors. Yet "there is a church apostolic of which the Church of England is a local presence and organ", declared Newman. In so saying he did not give much weight to the nineteenth Article of Religion which declares that the visible Church of Christ is a congregation of faithful men in which the pure word of God is preached and the Sacraments (two) "duly administered". That Article continues, "The Church of Rome," which Newman conceded in his Anglican days was also apostolic, "has erred not only in their living and manner of ceremonies, but also in matters of faith."

A petition signed by 7,000 clergy and 230,000 "heads of families" was drawn up and presented to the Archbishop. It spoke about the "consecration of and support of the established church", a Church which, it was not disputed, must obey each and every law relating to it or its worship sanctioned or ordered by Parliament. As a demonstration of churchmanship the manifestoes may have been heartening, but in the absence of any proposal to emancipate the Church of England from State control it was nugatory. An Evangelical or a Liberal church-man could conscientiously have signed it, possibly did. Next came the famous Oxford Tracts, the first by Newman himself —again the reference to "primitive" Christianity appears, the then refuge, it would appear, of Protestants and Anglo-Catholics alike. As the history of early Christian times had as yet scarcely been critically studied, any appeal to the primitive could be used for any cause. Newman, calling himself a "presbyter", not revealing his name, upholds the rights of Bishops (most of whom were Evangelicals or liberal). In the phrase "we encroach not upon the rights of the successors of the apostles", he builds his case for the clergy also on the apostolical descent, that "the sacred gift has been handed down to our present Bishops who have appointed us their assistants". What Newman here ignores is the distinction between orders and jurisdictions; that until the Reformation, apart from the sacerdotal sanction, the approval of the Pope was necessary to make a lawful Bishop and that now, though consecrated according to parliamentary Anglican ritual, in fact he is appointed by the King or his ministers. "Exalt our holy fathers the Bishops", he entreats, but most of those to be exalted denied or doubted whether they held that holy office which Newman would confer upon them. Indeed throughout the history of Anglo-Catholicism the ritualistic clergy have not hesitated to disobey their Evangelical or modernist Bishops.

The history of the Oxford Movement has been so often recounted that it is not proposed here to repeat it. It will be more profitable to endeavour to extract from its voluminous writings, sermons and contentions such cardinal principles as appear to have emerged in the course of its propaganda. Faced with the question: Where and what is the Church? Newman replies, and his answer was upheld by many of his followers, that the Church of England was a true branch of the undivided Catholic mystical body, of which the Roman was another part.

This theory, the Greek Church being added as a third con-stituent, is the basis of Anglo-Catholicism to this day. Yet is such a comforting doctrine sustainable? On the one side it is certain that the Catholic Church will have none of it. To quote Dom Aelred Graham, "It is the belief of Catholics that our Lord promised Peter a primacy of jurisdiction over His Church, a primacy which He actually conferred after His resurrection; they hold moreover that it was given not to Peter alone, but to the successors in his office and that it is vested for all time in the Roman Pontiff who is the visible head of the Church." And again, "The Church's doctrinal and jurisdictional authority is vested also in the Pontiff." Then, if we turn to the Anglican Ecclesiastical Constitution, we find that by statute the Crown is "Sovereign over all persons and causes ecclesiastical and temporal to the exclusion of any and every foreign power". The doctrines and worship of the Church of England were formulated and sanctioned by Statute; to alter them it is necessary to obtain parliamentary sanction for an Ecclesiastical measure of the National Assembly or to amend the Act of Uniformity of 1662. Convocation cannot even, with the most ample licence of the Crown, alter or repeal any one of the Articles or vary the rubric settled in the Prayer Book. But this constitutional objection to the theory that the Roman and Anglican Churches are part of an undivided body is only the least of obstacles to its acceptance; the spiritual and theological differences raise even greater difficulties, so great that one doubts whether the devout Anglicans who have sought a reunion have even now realised them. We have the admission of Newman, as an Anglican, that while he had closely studied the early fathers of the catholically inclined Anglican divines, he knew little of the actual tenets and practice of the Catholic Church. Years after, in his *Eirenicon*, Pusey also disclosed an amazing ignorance of the nature of the Catholic faith.

That there may be no mistake, I will confine myself to an accredited expositor of Catholicism: in the officially recognised *Teaching of the Church* it is declared that "it would be a pitiable mistake to think of the Body and Blood of Christ as a dead offering. It is a living offering and is offered by the living Christ. Christ is the priest of the Mass, it is Christ who celebrates it with a warm and living heart, the same heart with which He worshipped on Mount Calvary," and again, "Especially is the Catholic strong when he pleads before God the perfect sacrifice of Christ. Simply as a member of the Church, as a member of Christ's mystical body, every Catholic has a share in the sacrifice—and that partaking in the offering of the sacrifice is as real and far-reaching as is the Mystical Body itself." It is pointed out, in contrast, how "our lives are spent in the midst of men who, however religious-minded they may be, have lost all idea of sacrificial worship: the great Christian act of Sacrifice is no longer the centre of their religious observance". Moreover, as regards prayers for the intercession of the Saints, Catholics pray to the Angels and Saints, "not that through them God may know our petitions, but that through their prayers and merits our petitions may be effective (*ibid.*)". All this and more is irreconcilable on the theological as well as the legal plane with orthodox Anglican doctrine.

It was, doubtless, a feeling of the utter incompatibility of such essential Catholic teaching with the Thirty-Nine Articles to which he and other Anglican ministers and Oxford students had subscribed which constrained Newman in the famous Tract 90, regardless of the history and purpose to which they were directed, to show that the Lutheran and Calvinist principles there contained could be read without straining their grammatical sense to cover essential Catholic doctrine. His sincerity at the time was very unfairly questioned; what all must now realise, Catholic and Protestant alike, was the utter hopelessness of the task. By his conversion to the Catholic Church, Newman, of course, among other admissions, fully conceded this. Yet at the time he found himself boldly able to assert that the Articles could be interpreted "according to the sense of the Catholic Church". The Tract was published in February 1841. The underlying argument was that as the Articles were issued before the final sessions of the Council of Trent (1563), they could not be taken to be controverting them. The contention was an unsound one, as the Articles were without essential modification confirmed *after* the final Tridentine decrees, which they scarcely would have been had the Anglican Church not intended to give them their original meaning, but this consideration was by no means the only one upon which Newman relied. In any event, as Newman wrote, "the affair of No. 90 opened an entirely different scene". As was said by Lord Coleridge, a contemporary, "Four tutors protested, six doctors suspended, Hebdomadal boards censured, deans of college changed the dinner hour so as to make the hearing of Newman's sermon and a dinner in Hall 'incompatible transactions'." In the end after so many protests Newman wrote to his Bishop whom, consistently, he obeyed, that he would suspend the further publication of Tracts, but by that time thousands of copies of Tract 90 had been put into circulation.

The challenge had been made and the issues defined. Whatever the validity of the arguments, there is no doubt that the Tract was emphatically repudiated by the whole Anglican Church, save for the supporters of Newman, and this is what gives it such significance. Negatively it confirms the Protestant interpretation of the Articles which the Church of England had placed upon them in the past. As Coleridge related, within a fortnight of the publication four senior tutors at Oxford charged the writer with opening a means whereby men "might repudiate their obligations to the University". On March 15th, the Board of Heads of Houses declared that "the modes of interpretation suggested might be reconciled with the adoption of Roman Catholic error".

The vigorous support of the Tractarian W. G. Ward, who, differing from Newman, declared that he would construe the Articles in a "non-natural sense" (one wonders whether he knew of the Act of Charles I enjoining the contrary) added to the excitement and confusion. The Bishop of Oxford formally objected to the Tract; Newman resisted the suppression of the Tract on the condition above-mentioned, that no more should be published. Ward had admitted that the natural meaning of the Articles was evangelical and his "non-natural" interpretation cost him his lectureships. The final attempt to censure Tract 90 was at the time of Ward's degradation in 1843, but was prevented by veto of the Proctors. The general opinion is that if they had not intervened Oxford would formally have condemned it, and in doing so it would fairly have represented the opinion of the Church of England as a whole.

It remains to consider Tract 90 as such and its emphatic rejection as revealing the position in which the Anglicans stood, notwithstanding the Oxford Movement in 1841. The Tract, which is described as "Remarks on certain Passages in the Thirty Nine Articles", is stated in its introduction to have for its object "merely to show, that while our Prayer Book is acknowledged on all hands to be of Catholic origin, our Articles also, the offspring of an uncatholic age, are, through God's providence, to say the least, not uncatholic, and may be subscribed to by those who aim at being Catholic in heart and doctrine". There follows a close examination of the Articles, and the insistence on the later finality of the decrees of the Council of Trent already mentioned. Perhaps the most objectionable in the minds of Anglicans was the comment on Article twenty-eight that, while Transubstantiation as there defined is condemned, there is nothing to disallow "a real super-local presence in the Holy Sacrament". He declared that, properly construed, the Articles did not condemn prayers for the dead, the sacrifice of the Mass (only masses), nor belief in Purgatory; generally the case was that only current popular perversions of Roman Catholic doctrine were condemned by the reformers, but no Catholic doctrine as such. The Articles were to be construed as legal formularies and not as a basis of faith. Historically considered, his contentions were quite unsound, and Ward, as has been said, refused to accept his interpretation and, in effect, threw over the natural meaning of the words of the Articles altogether. Finally it must be said, lest any should think that the condemnation was purely an Oxford one, that the Anglican Bishops generally in terms condemned the tracts; Sumner of Chester expressed general Anglican opinion when he said that "those who sit in the reformers' seat have traduced the Reformation".

Next Pusey, who had preached a sermon on the Eucharist, alleged by his opponents to imply a belief in Transubstantiation and the sacrifice of the Mass—his actual words being that the Sacrament was a perpetual repetition of the sacrifice of Christ on the Cross—was impeached before a court of six doctors appointed by the Vice-Chancellor. In the result, Pusey was suspended from preaching within the University for two years. Though no reasoned judgment was given, it is clear that the doctrine of the sacrifice of the Mass was held by these Anglican theologians to be irreconcilable with the beliefs of the Church of England, and so, inferentially, was promulgated another condemnation of Anglo-Catholicism. But the final repudiation by the Anglicans of Newman's *Via Media* was illustrated in the condemnation of Ward in 1843, and the deprivation by the Convocation of Oxford of his degrees. His offence was the publication of the book called *The Ideal of a Christian Church considered in comparison with existing practice*; its gravamen was that he thought to see "the whole cycle of Roman doctrine gradually possessing numbers of English churchmen", yet it did not, while advocating ultimate submission to Rome, advise immediate joinder or submission. His catholically minded articles in the *British Critic* had already caused much perturbation, and the "ideal", which assumed that the Roman Church satisfied the conditions of a true church, while yet speaking of "the inherent vitality and powers of our own [the Anglican] Church", was not very understandable. He again declared that "in subscribing the Articles, I renounce no Roman doctrine", and he challenged ecclesiastical censure; it soon came.

First the book was examined by a committee of the Board of Heads of Houses, a body soon to be abolished by Parliament. They decided to submit to Convocation a condemnation of the book, a degradation of Ward by depriving him of his degrees, and finally a new declaration that in subscribing the Articles, a member of the University should declare that "he took them in the sense in which they were first published and were now imposed by the University". This last requirement was dropped; it was objected to as a new test. In effect, however, it represented truly the views of the great majority of the clergy who still took the Articles to mean what they said and even perhaps had some regard to historical and theological considerations. Thus, despite the pertinacity of Pusey and Keble, it must be conceded that the final result of the Oxford Movement, apart from detaching such men as Newman, Faber, Ward and their friends from the Anglican communion altogether in favour of the Catholic Church, of which they became such distinguished ornaments was to demonstrate beyond question in the mind of Oxford, the inherent Protestantism of the Church of England. The later developments, which have yet to be recorded, took place, for the most part, outside the ambit of University influence.

It might well be thought that, with the reception of Newman and so many others of the Oxford Movement into the Catholic Church, the internal troubles of the Anglicans, now recognisably Protestant, were at an end, and that they might now be allowed to relapse again into quiet somnolence, gradually ceasing to function save as the spiritual department of a highly laicised and indifferent society; but this was not to be. No sooner had the excitement of the Oxford rebellion subsided than a new issue was raised, this time in Devonshire, the subject being that of baptismal regeneration.

"In the year 1850," writes Purcell, in his *Life of Manning*, "there were two parties in the Church of England who held antagonistic opinions in matters of faith; professed antagonistic principles in regard to civil and spiritual authority as the government of the Church. The one party, calling itself Protestant, disbelieved in the sacramental system; and in the matter of Church government, it recognised as supreme not the Church but the State; not the spiritual, but the civil authority. The other party, calling itself Catholic, believed in the spiritual efficacy and divine origin of the Church; and denied to the civil power authority over matters of faith which they held by divine right and appointment to fall under the supreme authority of the spiritual power. The clergy belonging to either party had alike subscribed to the thirty-nine Articles and had taken the oath of supremacy."

To the latter of these, Gladstone, Manning, Hope and Robert Wilberforce belonged. It was the Gorham case, as it came to be called, which finally divided those who became Catholics in the full sense from their Anglican colleagues and altered the course of Church history by finally alienating Manning from the Church of England.

The cause itself raised two separate problems; first as to the doctrine of the Church of England on Baptism, and secondly the place of the secular courts of law in interpreting the significance of that Sacrament. The facts were as follows: The Reverend George Gorham, who on examination by the Bishop of Exeter was found to deny the doctrine of unqualified baptismal regeneration, although he had been ordained and signed the Articles which some maintained asserted it, was thereafter refused institution to the living of Bamford Speke, Devon, by the Bishop on the ground of heresy. Mr. Gorham appealed to the spiritual court, that of the Arches, to compel Dr. Phillpots to institute him, but Sir Henry Fust, the judge of that Court, decided in favour of the Bishop. There followed a further appeal by Mr. Gorham to the secular Privy Council sitting in its judicial committee. The Committee is admittedly a lay one, deriving from the Royal supremacy on its legal side, the Archbishops and Bishop of London on this occasion sitting with it, but only as assessors. The Committee without expressing their own views or doctrine found that baptismal regeneration was not, on grounds of construction of the Articles, a necessary belief in the Church of England, thus giving the victory to the low church anti-sacramental party.

That high church Anglicans should be perturbed at the

fact that the Privy Council adjudicated on the meaning of the doctrines of their Church may seem strange to those who do not realise how completely most of them had forgotten, or had not appreciated, the full implications of the royal supremacy. The acute Manning himself failed so to understand, until persuaded by Hope (afterwards Hope-Scott), the eminent lawyer, that the civil power since the Reformation had "usurped part of the Church's spiritual authority", and that "the Delegates sat under royal commission and the Privy Council represent the same authority". At length the future Cardinal also saw that "the Royal supremacy is in principle as old as Henry VIII".

The first statute of *Praemunire* of Edward III had been careful to confine its prohibition of causes taken "outside the King's court" to those "whereof cognizance pertains to that court", and at no time, until Henry VIII, had it been even claimed or suggested that the interpretation of Christian doctrine lay within the royal jurisdiction. By the 24th of Henry VIII, however, the Restraint of Appeals Act, all causes determinable by spiritual jurisdiction were to be decided in the King's courts, temporal or spiritual, and to be tried within the realm. They were to be determined by Commissioners appointed by the King. In ordinary cases the decisions of Archbishops however were to be final, but by a later Act, passed the next year, an appeal was granted from the Archbishops' court to a "High Court of Delegates in Ecclesiastical and Maritime causes". This Tribunal was re-established in 1583 and continued to sit until, in 1833, its functions were transferred to the new Judicial Committee of the Privy Council. Both the Henrician Court of Delegates and the Judicial Committee were equally secular and both derived their authority from the royal supremacy. Nothing in the Act of 1833 even made it necessary that a spiritual person should be a member of the Committee. There is power today in the Crown, by statute, to make rules for the attendance on the hearing of ecclesiastical causes of such Archbishops or Bishops as may be determined by such rules, but then only to sit as assessors. In practice only the Archbishops and the Bishop of London are sworn of the Privy Council.

In vain Manning tried to persuade the clergy to agree to agitate for an appeal court which would "carry with it the authority of the Church determining its own sphere". He, Robert Wilberforce and Mill, the Regius Professor of Hebrew at Cambridge, issued a declaration in which they said that they could not "acknowledge in the Crown the power recently exercised to hear and judge in appeal the internal state or merits of spiritual questions touching doctrine or discipline the custody of which is committed to the Church alone by the law of Christ" and circulated it to every beneficed clergyman and layman who had taken the oath of supremacy; but there was little or no response. Again to cite Purcell: "The vast and overwhelming bulk of the clergy of the Church of England, like the Bishops, by their silence or acquiescence, acknowledged the supremacy of the Crown in matters of faith"—and so it remains to this day; the Crown in Parliament settling the form of Anglican worship and doctrine and the Crown in Council determining the meaning of such and other laws affecting the spiritual life, doctrine and practice of the State National Church.

That this power of civil interpretation had always necessarily existed ever since the time of Henry, to be confirmed by the later Elizabethan settlement, is beyond dispute; a real novelty, more serious, was introduced by the Gorham decision in the latitude thereby afforded by the Judicial Committee to Anglican clerics to deny or modify the essential Catholic doctrine of baptismal regeneration. Up to that time it had been considered, though many Dissenters and Evangelicals disliked it on account of its sacramental nature, that all persons duly baptised are made regenerate by the Holy Spirit and that the remission of "original sin in and by the grace of baptism is an essential part of the article 'one baptism for the remission of sins' ", to quote from a declaration signed by Pusey as well as Manning and Robert Wilberforce, Hope, and many others at the time of the judgment.

According to the Evangelicals, Baptism, like other sacraments, is only efficacious if worthily received, but this, in the case of infants, could only be effected by a divine act of prevenient grace whereby the infant would notionally be endowed with faith and repentance. It follows that regeneration does not necessarily apply in every case where Baptism properly takes place—the Catholic view—but depends mysteriously on whether the infant does or does not receive that necessary prevenient grace which may, presumably, be limited to the predestined and elect. Thus, on the vital question of the validity of the Catholic view of the Sacrament, that whenever the Sacrament is validly conferred the baptismal character is given, an Anglican clergyman may, by law, apparently believe or disbelieve as he pleases, so construing, if he will, the benefits of Baptism in the words of Manning's declaration to be "uncertain and precarious".

Soon after this decision, in answer to which the Anglican Church as a body did nothing, Manning himself, the Church historian, Dr. T. W. Allies, Mr. Maskell, who had as Chaplain to the Bishop of Exeter examined Mr. Gorham and Mr. Dodsworth, the friend of Dr. Pusey, and many others joined the Catholic Church, with which momentous occurrence the history approximately of the third century of the Anglican Church ends, leaving its members in even greater confusion than before.

About this time the Church of England lost its last privileges at the Universities of Oxford and Cambridge. The test of the thirty-nine Articles subscription was ended for undergraduates and bachelors at Oxford (Cambridge being less insistent) in 1854, and in 1871 the declaration of Anglican belief for fellowships, etc., was also removed. In 1868 compulsory Church rates were abolished, and in 1869 the Anglican Church in Ireland was disestablished; to be followed in the twentieth century by that of Wales. Not until 1880 was the right of non-Anglicans to burial in churchyards finally conceded.

But far more serious, from a Christian standpoint, was the

legalisation of civil marriage in 1836 on a purely contractual basis, to be followed in 1857 by a general Divorce law. This latter was opposed vigorously by Bishop Wilberforce and Mr. Gladstone, but without success; it is to be noted that the then Archbishop of Canterbury and nine Bishops in the Lords supported, or, at least did not oppose, the bill. Once the principle of the inviolability of marriage was thus officially abandoned by the Church of England, though individuals might still hold the older, Catholic doctrine, there was nothing to prevent the grounds and facilities for divorce being increasingly enlarged, until, as Lord Russell of Killowen said in 1938 in the House of Lords, "What was once a holy estate enduring for the joint lives of the spouses is steadily assuming the characteristics of a tenancy at will."

The fact that, according to Anglican formularies, marriage is not an essential sacrament may have embarrassed the opponents to divorce who belonged to the Church of England. Today it may be said that among Catholics only is the sacramental view of marriage corporately and unequivocally maintained; but this is perhaps equally true of many other Christian institutions.

CHAPTER FIVE

THE FOURTH CENTURY

PART ONE

"AS the nineteenth century proceeded," comments H. A. L. Fisher in his *History of Europe*, "the stock of ideas, beliefs, and habits which European men had inherited from long-distant times underwent a profound transformation. History and scholarship, economics and physical science, the zeal of reforming prophets and the profuse ingenuity of mechanical inventors made of Europe in many respects a new society. In the Protestant half of Europe," he continues, "religious beliefs were shaped not so much on the authority of a developing Church as by the text of the Jewish and Christian scriptures—that ancient corpus of sacred literature was now subjected to minute examination."

As an example of this tendency, Matthew Arnold conceded the case against literal inspiration, when in his essays on *Religion and Dogma* he sought to justify the Bible solely on account of its effect on the religious imagination and did not attempt to defend its historical veracity.

Many other factors were at work to lessen the old uncritical belief. Astronomy, geology and, above all, the new evolutionary biology made the Protestant reliance on the factual accuracy of the account of the Creation in Genesis and other early biblical statements difficult to maintain. All alleged facts other than those capable of measurement and verification were discounted by Herbert Spencer, T. H. Huxley, J. Tyndall, G. J. Romanes and their associates in the new mode of thought as "unknowable". The reasons in logic for this relativity of judgment were emphasised long after by the "New Logic" of the Viennese school; the mind, they contended, was incapable of dealing with anything other than the relative world in flux with which it alone could and had to deal; all assertion about the Deity, and equally the denial of His existence, were not so much true or untrue as meaningless.

In so far as they had any philosophy, the Anglicans of the time accepted the logical principles of their opponents, such as Mill. "The two centuries long hatred of Roman Catholicism," comments Noel-Annan in his *Leslie Stephen* "had impaired the intellectual armament of the Church. Newman was accused of not putting the truth first because he employed a different kind of logic which was incomprehensible and repulsive to the Englishmen of his time. This absence of a comprehensive philosophical alternative hamstrung the defenders of the Church. Tied to the same tradition as the rationalists, they were without an adequate reply." The metaphysical and logical conflicts of Dr. Ward, the Catholic philosopher, with John Stuart Mill well illustrates the defensive difference between the Catholic and Anglican Churches of the time.

Confronted with these and other novel attacks, the method which found favour with many Churchmen was to ignore the whole problem and to endeavour to distract attention by attacks on Catholicism and Ritualists. Thus, while the foundations of evangelical theology were being undermined by biblical criticism, and a political revolution, largely atheistic, was spreading over Europe, the Puseyites, as they were now called, stunned by the recent conversions to Rome, were being bitterly denounced. The Prime Minister, Lord John Russell, thought fit to add to his attack on "papal aggression", occasioned by the creation of a Catholic hierarchy in England, even more violent diatribes against the "Ritualists" in the English Church.[1] He denounced their "mummeries of super-

---

[1] The need to make the declaration against Transubstantiation, etc., was removed in 1867 (30 and 31 Vict. c. 62), but a subsection arguably still applied to Catholics in certain reserved offices (e.g. Lord Chancellor). In 1871 a further act was passed, the effect of which is not very clear. Authorities differ as to the present position.

stition" and on November 4th, 1850, the Bishop of London, following his lead, in an episcopal letter complained of "those among my clergy who have thought themselves at liberty to imitate the forms and ceremonies of the Church of Rome". A great Protestant meeting to the same effect was shortly afterwards held, at which Lord Ashley (later Lord Shaftesbury) declared that he "would rather worship with Lydis on the banks of the river than with a hundred surpliced priests in the gorgeous temple of St. Barnabas"—an Anglo-Catholic church.

Here a Mr. Bennet officiated. Soon the Bishop wrote him, objecting to his use of the "eastward position", the presence of an assistant priest at the Celebration, and the use of the sign of the Cross—all these on the ground that they reminded the "weaker brethren of the abominations of popery". Incited, a mob entered the church every Sunday to create disorder and the incumbent's life was threatened. In 1851, after protracted disturbances, Mr. Bennet resigned his cure.

So violent was the general feeling that when Pusey attended the consecration of another Anglo-Catholic church at Plymouth he had to go under an assumed name. Yet Pusey habitually wore a plain black stole over a Surplice and never encouraged ceremonial and ornament; his chief offence was his advocacy of Confession. Even Ward in his Anglican days had been indifferent to ceremonial, as also was Newman. "It is plain to me," wrote J. E. Neale, an early Ritualist, "that the Tractarians missed one great principle, namely the influence of Aesthetics." He himself, in 1850, wore a Chasuble when celebrating Eucharist. Yet at this time even the Surplice was not to be tolerated, albeit the rubrics directed it to be worn. Riots occurred, notably at Exeter, and Evangelicals often refused to obey their Bishop's order to wear it.

Thus things went on while, to use the phrase of Wingfield Stratford, "orthodoxy crumbled".

High churchmen nevertheless pressed for the reopening of Convocation, last held in 1717. Lord Aberdeen, himself of their opinion, was now Prime Minister, and so, in 1853, the Convocation of Canterbury reassembled, though that of York was not allowed by its Archbishop to meet to transact business until 1861. Acrimony, however, was not abated by its meeting. In 1854 the Archdeacon of Taunton, Denison, was prosecuted for asserting the Eucharistic sacrifice in two sermons at Wells Cathedral and condemned in a diocesan court, though the proceedings were afterwards quashed as irregular. It is to be noted that, had he merely contented himself with a vindication of the Lutheran doctrine of the Real Presence without allusion to its sacrificial aspect, he would probably have escaped censure.

The judgments did not all go one way. On the Vicar of St. Paul's, Knightsbridge, being sued in 1855 to obtain the removal of a cross on the chancel screen, one behind the altar, the stone altar itself and altar candlesticks, the Privy Council, before which, somewhat inconsistently as an Anglo-Catholic, he had argued, decided that the altar frontals and the cross on the screen were legal, though ordering the removal of the other objected ornaments. It will be noted that the disputes had now shifted from doctrine to symbolic furniture, a significant change indicative of the failing interest in theology proper in the Anglican Church, and the disappearance of any consistent doctrine.

Ornaments being in part allowed, the use of Vestments followed; the Bishop of London objected, "no dresses", save the Surplice, might be worn, but Lowder, who esteemed himself a Catholic, defied his spiritual father in God and took refuge behind the secular law—could inconsistency go farther? "Marked disfavour should be adopted to those who promulgated principles likely to disturb the peace of the Church," said the Lutheran Prince Consort to Lord Aberdeen, and as from 1856, for nearly ten years Lord Palmerston had the recommendation of Bishops, and acted almost entirely on the advice of the ultra-evangelical Shaftesbury, it was not surprising that the Bench, with the exception of Hamilton and Philpotts, was entirely hostile to the Ritualists. They inhibited, reproved and in every way endeavoured to obstruct the introduction of Catholic practice or ceremonial. In particular they objected to the use of Confession, although the Courts

had held it lawful when not compulsory. There was some
reason on their side. The Anglican Liturgy had deliberately
removed Penance from its sacramental system. In the Catholic
Church a priest needs jurisdiction, conferred by the Bishop by
faculty, lawfully to act as confessor; outside the diocese a
priest has the power but cannot exercise it without definite
commission. So the whole process is carefully regulated, but
in the Anglican communion there is, of course, no such control. General absolution is recognised in the Liturgy, but the
sacrament of Penance and its consequent use in Confession is
officially unknown. Dr. Pusey, the great advocate of Confession, used to hear penitents in any parish he chose, and
Manning, in his Anglican days, gave absolution without even
the knowledge of his Diocesan. Despite the increasing use of
the confessional by Anglo-Catholics, it must be admitted that,
apart from special provision for the sick, it was entirely
irreconcilable in its full intent with the Anglican system.

In any case Confession was never practised except among
a very select group of Anglo-Catholics and, taking the Church
of England as a whole, had no support.

What is noticeable at the time is the entire lack of theological formulation or even intellectual defence against the
rapidly spreading agnostic arguments of Mill, Spencer and
Huxley. Compared with the Continental thinkers, de Maistre,
Montalembert, Lacordaire, Döllinger and Perrone, or the no
less famous English Ward and Newman, the Anglican Church
was intellectually almost impotent. In 1859, when the shattering
Origin of Species appeared, Ward pertinently observed, "Is
modern research going to prove that the biblical account of
creation is unscientific?" and the Anglican Church, save
perhaps by Wilberforce of Oxford, gave no coherent reply.

It was too readily assumed on all sides that the validity of
the Christian faith would depend upon certain speculations as
to the date of the creation of the world, but, as Belloc has
written, "A man's Faith may possibly be shaken by some
philosophical argument—though my own experience is that
when it is shaken, still more when it is lost, the cause at work

is not intellectual but always moral—the Faith is lost through wrongdoing. But that the Faith could conceivably be lost through not being able to define at what exact moment true man appeared, is to me quite inconceivable."

Nevertheless, at the time these and other secular arguments and criticisms had great weight and led at last to the loss of millions from the Church of England (and from Nonconformity), so that today, as has been said, it is doubtful whether many more than two of the 48,000,000 of the inhabitants of England are actively associated with the National Church. In the face of such loss of definite belief, the adoption of ritual and ceremony, without canonical or episcopal sanction, arbitrarily selected from Roman sources to illustrate doctrines often incompatible with Anglican rubric at the whim of particular clerics, must be admitted to have been of doubtful utility. Not by such means could the agnostic tendency of the Victorian age be arrested.[1]

For now it was, when Christianity itself, humanly speaking, was in debate, that the absence of dogmatic authority in the Church of England manifested itself in a way which had not been so marked at a time when the mass of people, however indolent and unresponsive, had yet shown themselves vaguely to be believers. The appeal of the Anglo-Catholics was in the main to the wealthy—one notes the proximity of many of their churches to Mayfair and seaside resorts,[2] and to the very poor in the slums, where they did much heroic work. Nevertheless with most English the negative suspicion of Ritualists and Catholics had largely taken the place of any dogmatic creed. Dislike of

> The wily, crafty Ritualist
> With cope and incense strong,
> This unctuous and bearded priest
> With broidered vestments long,

---

[1] In 1851, out of 18,000,000, but 7,261,032 went to church on a particular Sunday; slightly above half were Anglican.

[2] Dean Inge called it, after the railway, a "London, Brighton and South Coast religion".

as a contemporary verse has it, was often the extent of his religion.

Nevertheless attempts were made to cope with the rising tide of doubt. This took two forms, for appeal to an authoritative Church was, by common consent, barred out. The one sought to show that recent scientific knowledge was consistent with biblical cosmology; the other, the more permanent, to attempt to reconcile the Bible with recent discovery.

As to the first, we have to admit that it was of a very inadequate order. The story of the older Gosse, a considerable geologist who, nevertheless, in his *Omphalos* sought to counteract the influence of Lyell's geological history of man by contending that when Creation took place the world arose with all the structural appearance of a planet on which life had long existed—described by irreverent journalists as an attempt to show that God had hid the fossils to tempt scientists into infidelity—is but one example of a defence doomed to failure. Samuel Kinns' later *Moses and Geology* was equally inconclusive.

The essential weakness of these apologists was that the truth of biblical cosmology was made to depend upon alleged "evidences"—a heritage of the "Evidences" of Paley; till a recent time still compulsory for certain university examinations. Thus it was argued that the failure to show that one species could change into another was conclusive of the special creation of each by God. Side by side with all this persisted the hatred of Rome. We take, for example, the apologetic work *The Church before the Flood* by a clergyman and doctor of divinity, Cumming, who declared, against Romans and agnostics alike, that Abel was slain by his brother because he was a Protestant, or the *Horae Apostolicae* of Elliott, which was written to show that the Apocalypse was directed against popery.

Thus the appeal to the infallible authority of the Catholic Church being violently rejected, and the evangelical attempts to reconcile Genesis and geology failing to produce conviction, it only remained to attempt to effect a reconciliation by

adapting the Faith to the "modern situation"; to use a phrase
employed in a later eirenicon, *Foundations*.

This task was sought to be achieved in a book of essays by
various authors eminent in the Anglican Church called *Essays
and Reviews*. It was published in 1860. It was not well received.
Two of the authors were subsequently prosecuted for heretical
views on the inspiration of Scripture, Justification and
Eternal Punishment. Though the Judicial Committee of the
Privy Council, true to its tolerant form, acquitted them of legal
heresy, they were nevertheless censured in both Houses of
Convocation in 1864; so now it appeared that the bewildered
Anglican Church spoke officially with two voices, the King in
Council being contradicted by his more spiritual assembly.
One is tempted to ask, in such circumstances, what authority
still rested in the King as Supreme Governor, speaking
judicially through his appointed organ, of which he was also
Governor, when Convocation rejected the conclusions of the
Judicial Committee?

Before this final remonstrance, an agitation against the
writers had been steadily growing in clerical circles. Some
were denounced as "Positivists", and in 1861, at a meeting at
Lambeth, twenty-five Bishops had expressed "the pain which
it had given them that any clergyman should have expressed
such opinions not consistent with an honest subscription to
the formularies of our Church, with many of the fundamental
doctrines of which they appear to be at variance".

The decision of the Privy Council was that "no verbal
contradictions between the impugned statements and the
formularies of the Church had been established".

A similar controversy arose out of the expressed opinions
of Dr. Colenso, Bishop of Natal, a diocese in the new province
of South Africa. He, apparently, had been influenced by
prevailing tendencies in religious thought, and in 1862, after
he had published a commentary on the Epistle to the Romans,
in which he denied that he found any evidence to support
a privileged covenanted Church, proceeded to issue his
Critical Examination of the Pentateuch, not completed until

1866. There he not only denied much of the history of the first five books of the Bible, but went on to say that as a consequence he could no longer ordain priests in the form in which the literal truth of the Bible is asserted, nor use the baptismal service because it assumed the reality of the Flood. He criticised also the books of Leviticus and Numbers, and generally accepted much of the criticism of the Scriptures which was then being made, particularly in Germany. The taunt of Disraeli that "he commenced his theological studies after he had grasped the crozier" was two-edged; many of the Bishops, it is feared, never commenced their theological studies at any time.

Other Colonial Bishops inhibited Dr. Colenso from preaching in their dioceses and finally he was tried before the Metropolitan, Bishop Gray, at Capetown in 1863 and deprived for heresy. Then the matter came before the Privy Council. They decided a matter which went beyond the immediate dispute, namely that the Crown, in that the Cape of Good Hope had self-government, had exceeded its powers in setting up the sees of Capetown and Natal. All that now could be done was for the Colonial Bishopric Fund to refuse to pay Bishop Colenso his stipend, but this also was held by the Master of the Rolls to be illegal as Colenso was still in law Bishop of Natal and entitled under the Trusts to be paid accordingly. Thus to the very serious dissensions as to fundamental Christian dogmas was added the difficult question of the jurisdiction of the Church of England as by law established overseas. It had been decided by Coke, and accepted by the Privy Council in the case above referred to and in an earlier one, that the Crown cannot establish episcopal sees outside the realm, for there, apart from local legislation, only the common law obtains, and this, of course, has nothing to do with spiritual jurisdiction. In practice, in so far as a Colonial Bishop is consecrated, generally, by the Archbishop of Canterbury in England, it is usual for the Crown to issue a licence for such consecration on the petition of the Archbishop. The licence is even more Erastian in form than that of an English Bishop in that in terms it "authorises and empowers" the Archbishop to consecrate and "execute all and singular those things which belong to your pastoral office in respect of such consecration". The power of the Crown over the Church, even in its pastoral activities, could not be more strongly expressed.[1]

This was a period of much litigation. In 1860 a Fellow of Cambridge, a Mr. Heath, was prosecuted for denying the propitiation wrought by the sacrifice of Christ and failed to retain his living, even on appeal to the Privy Council; he had gone too far. Next, Voysey, who seceded and formed a new church, preached so "modernist" a sermon, which he afterwards published, that he also was deprived and similarly failed in the Privy Council. There followed, written by a layman, Professor Seeley, a book, *Ecce Homo*, dealing with Christ as a man among His fellows, rather on the same lines as the notorious *Vie de Jésu* of Renan. His belief in the divinity of our Lord was not clearly stated, and in this he followed the trend of the Broad Church generally; imperceptibly to become more and more heretical. It was this tendency which brought about a demand for the abolition of the compulsory recital at certain seasons of the so-called Athanasian Creed, or at least for its optional use. The Ritual Commission of 1870 recommended that the rubric which requires it to be said should contain a note to the effect that "the condemnations in this confession of faith are to be nowise understood than as a solemn warning of the peril of those who wilfully reject the Catholic faith", but nothing came of it. Every year in Convocation, for a long time, the matter was brought up, the broad churchman, Dean Stanley, urging its total disuse, but though the lower House made a synodical declaration on it nothing was done.

It was probably during the Arian controversies in Gaul in the fifth century that this creed came into existence and by the

[1] In 1841 George Augustus Selwyn, about to be consecrated to be Bishop of New Zealand, had to protest against a statement in his Letters Patent that the Crown gave him "power to ordain"; and the latitude and longitude of the portion of the Pacific Ocean within his jurisdiction were determined by Act of Parliament.

ninth century it was employed in England. By the tenth it had been adopted by the whole Catholic Church. Luther acclaimed it, calling the creed "a bulwark of the Apostles' one". Why then should the broad churchmen of Victorian times be so anxious for its removal? It is to be noted that in the Protestant episcopal churches of Ireland and America it is discounted; in the American Prayer Book it is omitted altogether and in Ireland no longer recited. The Archbishop of Canterbury at Convocation in 1871 defended it, chiefly on the ground that it was of use among the heathen, but the fact is that in its explicit clauses it expressly excludes from the Catholic faith all those who were ambiguous or evasive about the nature of the Trinity, as were many who wished for its removal. As to the "damnatory" clauses, it was sought to be said in 1869, as a new rubric, to apply to those only who deny the substance of the Christian religion and not infallibly to everyone who may be in doubt as to the meaning of a particular article. The creed was defended in a sermon by Dr. Pusey in that sense in 1873.

But although Convocation and the Bishops remained steadfast in the matter of the Athanasian Creed, they still waged a relentless war with their fellow high church Anglicans.

The discussion about the Athanasian Creed was, perhaps, the last time that the Church of England, as a corporate body, considered directly any question of doctrine until the passing of the revised Prayer Book in 1927 by the Convocations and National Assembly. For the most part, their attention was now directed solely towards ritual vestments and ornaments, things which in themselves do not necessarily have any definite doctrinal significance.

The early disturbances were surpassed in 1860 when the "reader" appointed by the vestry of St. George's in the East, at the docks, a strong Evangelical, organised opposition to the ritualistic missionaries selected by the Vicar. A mob took possession of the church on more than one occasion, the offence being a choral Communion and the use of Vestments. In the end the Vicar, on the persuasion of Dr. Stanley, temporarily retired, but so much trouble had arisen there and elsewhere that the lower House of the Canterbury Convocation decided to consider the six disputed points: Vestments, Altar lights, Incense, Elevation of the Host, Non-communicating attendance and Wafer Bread. They agreed with the Bishops that "no alteration should be made in churches until the sanction of the Bishop had been obtained".

Then, after Lord Shaftesbury had failed to pass a prohibitive Clerical Vestments Bill, the whole matter was sent to a Royal Commission.

By the time this met, however, more lawsuits had been heard. In *Martin v. Mackonochie*, the Dean of Arches gave a judgment not wholly favourable to either side, but the Privy Council decided against the high church defendant on all points; Ritualism had been, in substance, condemned. In *Purchas v. Elphinstone*, also heard first in the Court of Arches, Vestments, the Eastward position, Wafer Bread and the Mixed Chalice were upheld, again all to be reversed in the Judicial Committee. The impeached clergy as a whole ignored these decisions. On the insistence of the Queen, Mr. Gladstone being the chief opponent, there was passed the Public Worship Regulation Act 1874, "for facilitating, expediting and cheapening proceedings in enforcing clergy discipline". In the final form the Bishop had a veto on all proceedings, and the Archbishops were empowered, subject to the approval of the Crown, to appoint a judge who must be a member of the Church of England to hear complaints with regard to alterations in the fabric or ornaments in the Church or in the ritual prescribed in the book of Common Prayer, but, again, he could only act if the Bishop was of opinion that proceedings should be taken.

The Lower House of Convocation protested but was ignored. By a galling coincidence the Judge of the Divorce Court—a peculiarly uncatholic tribunal—was appointed the first Judge. Under its provisions several clergy were actually imprisoned for contempt, and in 1876 the Vicar of St. Peter's, Folkestone, was charged witht he old offences of the Eastward position, Vestments, Wafer Bread and the erection of a Crucifix on the Rood Screen. The Judge decided against him on all these matters, but the Judicial Committee of the Privy Council allowed the appeal as to the Eastward position but not otherwise. Nevertheless for the most part, despite much more litigation, the Anglo-Catholic ritual continued, indeed spread rapidly.

So far we have been concerned rather with the doctrines and practice of the Anglican Church than with its social teaching. Here, as with other denominations, a difference of outlook developed between those who were actively concerned for a Christian state of society as such and those who would seek salvation solely in individual piety. The two interests were not inconsistent, but the emphasis laid on one or the other motives is important.

In the middle ages men were scarcely conscious of this possible incompatibility. St. Thomas, for example, wrote on theology and social politics as if they were indivisible. The Eternal Law, he stresses, is reflected in the Natural, which in its turn should find expression in the municipal laws of each State. This doctrine still forms the foundation of Catholic sociology. The laws of the Church, often embodied in the legislation of the secular state forbidding usury and economic oppression, enforcing the principle of the fair wage and encouraging co-operation in the guild system, are all illustrations of the application of this principle.

"The Puritan movement," says Thorold Rogers, "was essentially one of the middle classes, of the traders in the towns and the farmers in the country." They gave their money to the cause of Parliament against Charles I, and were among the founders of the Bank of England and other commercial institutions. The principal business in most of the towns of England was by the seventeenth century in the hands of Nonconformists or Anglicans who held the same commercial and theological opinions. It was the monied Whigs and their friends who financed the revolution of 1688; the high church-men being of the old feudal landed class and their dependants.

Thus the objection to Wesley, who, since the days of the

Lollards and Levellers, had been one of the first to appeal to the labouring man and so restore his dignity, was as much social and economic as theological; he, unlike the earlier commercial Puritans, could readily be represented at the outset of his preaching as a political agitator, but very soon his movement became respectable. During the earlier part of the nineteenth century the religious appeal for social justice came, it is now generally recognised, from a small group of Anglicans. F. D. Maurice, who was a theologian, and Kingsley, who was not, were associated in a movement to "christianise the Socialists and socialise Christianity", bearing in mind that Socialism in the minds of these men meant something very different from later Fabian or Social Democratic secular conceptions.

Kingsley, of the Christian Socialists, as they called themselves, alone foresaw how mass production would deprive the ordinary operative of his personal dignity and status, an evil which modern commercialism or Communism has done nothing to remove. In 1862 he wrote "that large bodies of men should be employed day after day in exclusively performing some minute operation is to me shocking". Like all other churchmen of that time who departed from purely clerical functions, he aroused hostility, though not so much as Maurice, his colleague, who was attacked on theological as well as on social grounds.

The melancholy fact is that the Anglican hierarchy and clergy as a whole, even during the worst oppressive period of the industrial revolution, were indifferent or hostile to all schemes for the social regeneration of the dispossessed. Thus when Kingsley preached to working men who had come to see the Great Exhibition in 1851 that "the business of a Christian priest is to preach freedom, equality and brotherhood in the fullest, deepest sense", and so forth, he was censured by the then Bishop of London who forbade him again to preach in the diocese. A meeting of protest was held on Kennington Common, when it was suggested that, like Wesley, he should start a free Church of his own. His refusal to dogmatise about the pains of Hell added to the opponents of his social theories the suspicions of the Evangelicals. Not even his violent anti-Catholic sentiments could fully restore him to their confidence.

But more influential than he was Frederick Maurice, according to Dr. Raven "of all the churchmen of the nineteenth century—incomparably the greatest". "The Kingdom of God," Maurice declared, "is to me the one great existing reality which is to renew the earth." On this foundation was built the whole of his sociology, which was thus through and through religious in inspiration. His attempt to form trade associations to encourage co-operation in industry was but one instance of a remedy for his fear that "the whole disease of money getting and money worship by which we have been so long tormented, must end in death". To quote Maurice Reckitt in his Scott-Holland lectures, "As the golden age of Victorian capitalism settled down upon the country in the sixties, Maurice became, unlike almost all of his contemporaries, not less, but more alarmed about the moral foundations of nineteenth-century capitalism."

Although perhaps we are not here directly concerned, it is important to observe that Cardinal Manning in the Catholic Church was coming to a similar conclusion. In 1880, in his pastoral letter to his clergy, he was moved to write: "In the midst of immeasurable wealth is a want which the poorest country in Europe scarcely knows. We have in the midst of us not poverty alone—but also pauperism. The inequalities of our social state unless they be redressed by humility and charity, sympathy and self-denial are dangerous to society." Ward also, much earlier, while he was yet nominally an Anglican, in his *Ideal of a Christian Church*, turning for the moment from the exposure of the doctrinal deficiencies of Anglicanism to social justice, wrote, "England is a vast mass of festering misery and discontent." He draws the conclusion against the Church of England that "a pure Church could not have co-existed with such tremendous evils". Finally he says, "Ever since the schism of the sixteenth century the English

Church has been swayed by a spirit of arrogance, self-content-ment and self-complacency." It is not surprising that a then Anglican University should deprive him of his degrees!

*   *   *   *   *

Another, and quite different, matter (the consideration of which will often recur) was raised in the growing desire after the Oxford Movement of some Anglo-Catholics to seek reunion with the Apostolic See. Discussions of this matter had been intermittently carried on in the time of Charles I and again after the French Revolution, but in 1857 a specific society was formed, called the Association for the Promotion of the Unity of Christendom, which published an address from some two hundred of the Anglican clergy to the Pope asking for consideration of the subject. They were encouraged by some few Catholics, such as Mr. Ambrose de Lisle, and produced a paper called the *Union Review*. It was thought in Rome that the Anglicans still toyed with the idea, once taught by Newman, that there were in the world today three branches of a divided Catholic Church, the Roman, Greek and Anglican, and on this head alone their petition stood condemned.

To this they answered that they had been misunderstood, moreover they added that they had "cultivated a good feeling towards the venerable Church of Rome", which they felt should not go unacknowledged. On the main issue, they declared that they only contended that there were three churches *de facto* but not *de jure*, but, as Manning pointed out, this denied the "exclusive unity of the Catholic and Roman Church and its exclusive infallibility and the universal duty and necessity of submission to it". Finally the Holy Office at Rome issued letters to the Catholic Bishops in England saying that the unity of the Church was absolute and has never been lost, that Christ is indefectible, not only in duration but in doctrine; that the primacy of the Visible Head is of divine institution and that the Catholic and Roman Church alone has received the name of Catholic and that to say otherwise is manifest heresy. Cardinal Manning very truly described the position of the petitioners when he said that "the Church of England represents about half the English people, and the Anglican [i.e. Anglo-Catholic] school represents only a portion of the Church of England and the Unionist movement represents only a fraction of that section". Nevertheless he congratulated himself in his first pastoral letter as Archbishop in 1865 that such "an association should exist—a fact new in our history since the separation of England from Catholic unity—a change has visibly come over England", though he goes on, "there is still much hostility or stagnant ignorance". Later the matter was raised by the late Lord Halifax on two occasions, again, inevitably, without result.

The prevailing religious contentions were increased by the introduction into Parliament in 1870 of an Education Bill. As long ago as 1843, on the educational clauses of a Factory Bill, the then Prime Minister had told Lord Lyttelton that he "was not prepared to limit Church teaching in schools to the exposition of Scripture". In 1853 Mr. Gladstone had approved the "system of separate and independent subsidies to various religious denominations", and by 1870 half of the elementary schools were controlled by the Church of England. The question was whether, in return for government assistance, they would admit any element of "undenominationalism". This was what the Nonconformists wanted. In 1855 they had already desired the Scriptures to be read in schools "excluding all catechisms and formularies of Faith", and this is the policy which Mr. Gladstone's Government now adopted. This new policy was to include religion and exclude dogma and this was attempted to be solved by a provision that in all public elementary schools attendance at religious service should not be made obligatory and that a parent could withdraw his child. Moreover in the new Board Schools, as they were then called, it was specifically required by the "Cowper-Temple" clause that no "catechism or religious formulary distinctive of any denomination" should be taught. This did not content the

Radicals (nor curiously many of the Nonconformists), most of whom wished for a completely secular system. It is difficult to believe that Wesley, Whitfield or any of their generation would not have been horrified at such a suggestion. The Anglicans, with reservations, supported the seductive compromise of Cowper-Temple that there should be Bible reading in the Board Schools, but no distinctive formulary; as Disraeli said, what they wanted was full religious education in the Church Schools, and for the moment they retained it. Their argument to abandon denominational teaching, save in Church Schools, is understandable; as late as 1895 there were no less than 70,000 more children in the Church than the Board Schools, and in many rural areas the Anglican school was the only one. As has been said by a modern historian, Wingfield Stratford, somewhat cynically, "In the new State-aided Board Schools, the Scriptures were allowed to be taught provided they were not explained with sufficient clarity to allow the explanation to coincide with anyone's doctrine." Truly, as that author comments, "Orthodoxy was in retreat."

There can be no doubt, the Catholics saw it clearly, that the Church of England, by supporting so disastrous a compromise from a religious point of view, did much to assist in the bringing up of an entirely secular agnostic generation. Their schools, for financial reasons, were gradually being handed over to the local authorities and by 1902 they had realised the full nature of their earlier error.

Apart from the loss of their denominational teaching, the old benefactions were proving insufficient to keep the voluntary religious schools up to the modern requirements of efficiency. The Government therefore was at length persuaded to attempt to place all schools, whether denominational or not, on the rates; the county or county borough to be the authority, superseding the School Boards. The Nonconformists and Liberals immediately raised the cry of "The Church (and Rome) on the Rates!" Nevertheless the bill of 1902 became law; it placed the maintenance of the Voluntary Schools on public finance. The denominations were to be responsible for

I

repairs and they would provide the sites and buildings. Subject to this the schools would be maintained by the local authority. As to teachers, they were to be appointed by the managers, with a veto on educational grounds by the local education authority. Secular education was to be under the local authority; religion controlled by the managers. It was in part a defeat for the Nonconformist and secular parties. Led by Dr. Clifford, some Dissenters refused to pay their rates and in Nonconformist counties tried to obstruct the working of the Act. Though, when the Liberals were returned in 1906, they tried to upset the system, they failed,[1] even with statutory aid the Anglican and Nonconformist Church Schools still were unable to maintain their independence. An agreed syllabus of religious instruction, in which surrender, of course, Catholics took no part, was negotiated in many places and agreement was reached for it to be used in all Council Schools—and on this understanding many more Voluntary Schools were surrendered to the authority. So it was that, while before 1870 every school was voluntary, the number of Anglican and Dissenting ones now fell from 12,000 odd at the time of the passing of the 1902 Act to about 10,000 in 1948, of which under 200 were of the Free Churches.

Finally, by an Act of 1936, the local authority was given power to pay up to three-quarters of the cost of refurbishing denominational schools, the condition being that the "agreed syllabus was to be used for those (in practice non-Catholic) whose parents desired it"; the concession was limited to senior schools. By 1938 there were practically no boroughs in England without a Catholic School. Thus, as Mr. Beales has written, there were coming to be "two mutually exclusive systems, one Catholic and one secular"—as Lord Quickswood had prophesied in 1902, Mr. Allies in 1883, Manning in 1870 and W. G. Ward a century ago.

Here we are concerned only with the effect of this policy

[1] Three Education Bills, 1906 (Birrell), 1907 (McKenna), 1908 (Runciman), were thrown out by the Lords. They were all designed to discourage the Voluntary Schools.

of pusillanimity which is destroying the possibility of distinctive Anglican training for the young and has merged it in vague scriptural lessons which Nonconformists can accept. It is too soon to estimate this abandonment of all high church or Anglo-Catholic teaching; what is certain is that, unless a change is made, the majority of children in England, who are not Catholic, will in future grow up without any definite religious ideas or education whatever, save what their parents, similarly ill-educated, may supply.

Returning to matters more immediately ecclesiastical, the refusal of some of the prosecuted Anglo-Catholic clergy to recognise the Court set up under the 1874 Act, resulting in five of them going to prison rather than admit the jurisdiction, caused some revulsion in favour of the Ritualists, so that, in 1881, the high church Dean of St. Paul's was able to present a petition signed by over 5000 clergy asking first that "a widely divergent ritual practice" be permitted and also that "the conscientious obedience of clergy who believe the Church to be of divine appointment" be obtained by a modification of the law.

It was tardily admitted that the Public Worship Regulation Act, in setting up a lay tribunal to deal with clerical offences, had been a failure, and in the same year there was constituted a Royal Commission to enquire into the working of Ecclesiastical Courts. It recommended, among other things, a joint Appeal Court other than the Privy Council, but Evangelical Bishops continued to harass high church clergy by refusing licences and the Protestant Church Association continued its prosecutions. They culminated in the trial of the Bishop of Lincoln—no Bishop had yet been attacked—before the Archbishop, Benson. The Court had not sat for two hundred years and its jurisdiction was very uncertain, but at any rate it was not secular. In the event, Dr. E. King, Bishop of Lincoln, appeared before the Archbishop and five episcopal assessors. After an interval of nearly nine months the judgment was given. While objecting to certain practices, it decided that the "Eastward position, the manual acts being visible, was legal, so also ablutions, the use of two altar lights and the singing of the *Agnus Dei*". On appeal the competence of the Judicial Committee was denied by the Bishop, but in the result they upheld the spiritual court.

The words of a learned Catholic priest, Mgr. Moyes, are informative of general opinion at the time. It had been declared in the English Church Union (the Anglo-Catholic association) that the Archbishop had no spiritual jurisdiction to try the Bishop of Lincoln, and that the "Synod of the Province" is the only competent tribunal for the purpose.

> "It will be remembered," he says, "that the one point which the Archbishop has decided is that he has jurisdiction and that his Court is the proper tribunal. The 136 incumbents, however, review and reverse this, his first decision.
>
> This first resolution suggests a very far-reaching enquiry. Where is the living authority or Court which can decide what is or is not within the Archbishop's jurisdiction? I say 'living authority', for dead authorities, such as canons and decrees of early councils, obviously require authoritative application and interpretation, so that the question only repeats itself until we find a Court or actual authority to apply, interpret, and enforce them."

The second proposition stated that the Archbishop, by admitting the spiritual authority of the Privy Council, has deprived his judgment of all spiritual validity. The learned Canon comments:

> "Taken seriously, such a resolution has an ominous significance. It logically means that Anglicanism will regard as null and worthless all future judgments from Lambeth, until an Archbishop can be found who will claim spiritual jurisdiction, distinct from and independent of the authority of the Crown, as exercised through the Privy Council. That practically amounts to a self-granted dispensation from ecclesiastical obedience."

After the judgment had been delivered, Mgr. Moyes further commented:

"Everybody knows—but by tacit agreement nobody apparently dares to speak his thought—that the whole of this trial is a battle, not of ritual, but of belief. The Church Association, and all that section of the Establishment which for the purposes of the late trial was labelled 'Read and Others', know perfectly well in their heart of hearts that when they attacked the Bishop of Lincoln it was not that they cared a button of his cassock whether he stood eastward or westward, or mixed his chalice, or lighted his candles; but what does matter to them, and matter much, is that he should seek to do what they are determined he shall not, namely, bring back the doctrine of the Mass and Transubstantiation into the Church of England in reversal of the work of the Reformation. And the Bishop who is thus attacked knows equally well that it is not the symbols, but the doctrines which underlie the symbols, that are at stake in his impeachment. The Archbishop, who sits in judgment upon both, knows it better than either, and all England knows it with him. Then upon this basis of knowledge we have a long public trial extending over several weeks, learned counsel pleading for days at a time, the Archbishop maturing his decision for months, and then producing a judgment which requires no less than five hours to deliver. And yet, in all the indictments, in the pleadings, in the judgment, never even once is the question of belief directly alluded to! Belief is the question which is at the root of the whole proceedings. It is the question which alone is of synodical importance. It is the question which is deepest in everybody's heart and uppermost in everybody's mind. And yet, by common consent, all agree quietly to pass it over untouched and unmentioned, and fight the whole battle, if battle must be fought, over such wretched counters as minutiae of rubrics and ritual."

These remarks are here quoted, not by way of denigration of the Church of England, but to illustrate the fact that the spiritual court, which reasonably might have been expected to deal with doctrine, approached the problem from precisely the same angle as did the Privy Council, namely by the close examination of decrees and precedents, mostly derived from the pre-Reformation Church, and applied the ordinary principles of legal interpretation to those documents. Not for a moment was the question of principle allowed to emerge.

As the Anglican *Guardian* wrote at the time, "the Secretary of the Church Association declared that the feeling that the Archbishop can make the Adoration of the Host harmless by saying that the rites which express it mean nothing at all, can hardly be sustained. He might as well pronounce that ice does not freeze, nor fire burn". The Anglican Bishop of Gloucester and Bristol most acutely pointed out in a pastoral:

"It is impossible to deny that there are usages and ceremonies which are intimately connected with doctrine, and are tenaciously maintained, and just as tenaciously opposed, because both parties know that doctrine is the moving principle. Such usages will never be disposed of by the declaration that they are to be understood to have no doctrinal significance. Neither party will admit this and controversy will continue with even increased asperity. In attempting to lay down limits of ritual, limits of doctrine will commonly have, in some form or other, to be regarded as a part of the problem, and it is idle to think it can be otherwise."

It had been said that the Lambeth judgment made for peace, on which hope Dr. Bell, an Anglican clergyman, in contradiction, wrote:

"I cannot imagine how the Judgment makes for peace. When in common life two parties quarrel and through the action of a friend are reconciled, they confess their sorrow for the past, shake hands and resolve to put away the causes of offence from which the quarrel sprang. There is now peace between them, and they are in all points at one. Has this any parallel in the present case? Will high churchmen now confess they were wrong in disturbing the peace of the Church for the sake of introducing ceremonial pronounced by both Courts to have no doctrinal significance? Will they abandon ritual so meaningless, or even acknowledge that it has no doctrinal import whatever? Will Evangelical men acknowledge that they have been mistaken in objecting to ceremonial borrowed from the Roman Church and used because of its doctrinal significance? Will they look upon it with any greater favour than before and perhaps adopt it since it has been declared not to be illegal? I cannot think so, and I believe they will avoid, as before, churches where such unmeaning and objectionable ritual is practised. Instead of bringing high churchmen and Evangelical churchmen nearer to one another, I believe it will accentuate their differences."

CHAPTER SIX

THE FOURTH CENTURY

PART TWO

THE victory, in the political field, of Liberalism and Labour in 1906 marks the end of an epoch in Church matters as well as in secular. For the preceding hundred years the basic characteristic of English life had been devotion to commerce, and the prevailing Evangelical individualistic morality of the time had spread far beyond its actual religious devotees. The idea, though the ugly fact was disguised by phrases, that to succeed in the fight for wealth was the reward of a good man and that to sink into or remain in poverty was a sign of sin was fortified by Old Testament texts.[1] The doctrine of election was not without influence here; although to some extent a man might improve his position by his own efforts, often of a judicious self-regarding kind, yet a mysterious fate, not without authority from the Deity, placed a man in a state of society where he would inherit, or be in a position to exploit, a favourable financial situation. Others were condemned, *ab initio*, to economic subordination, frustration or failure—to doubt this was almost an act of impiety.

Here Science and Religion could meet; the doctrine of the Survival of the Fittest endorsed the view that the race was for the strong; Calvin had been justified by Darwin; all that was needed was to exclude those views alleged to be socialistic, whether derived from mediaeval Catholicism or from modern reformers, which would extend the function of Charity to the whole of human life, regarding us in a true sense as brothers, and no longer continue to limit the term to almsgiving or grudging Poor Law assistance.

[1] "Prosperity is the blessing of the Old Testament; adversity the blessing of the New."—FRANCIS BACON.

The new protest against this Victorian teaching, whether in Evangelical form or otherwise, was not confined to churchmen; it had already been made, stridently, by the followers of Marx, and, in a more moderate way, by the Fabians, and by Maurice, Kingsley, Ruskin and Carlyle. In the Catholic Church, as we have seen, Cardinal Manning had questioned the whole structure of plutocratic society, for this is what was developing out of the more respectable Victorian capitalism, and new names were springing up in the high church: Scott Holland, James Adderley, Stuart Headlam, Conrad Noel, Bishop Gore and others who individually, and in the Christian Social Union, criticised anew the whole structure of "acquisitive society" from a Christian standpoint.

All this rediscovery, for it had largely been forgotten since the Middle Ages, of the social nature and obligations of man was fatal to the old Protestantism. Though religion is the key to all other problems in a carnal world (as Manning once told Hilaire Belloc), yet its actual expression is influenced to a considerable extent by the prevailing habits of the men to whom it is preached or who practise it. Individualism in religion flourishes when Society is atomic in its assumptions; once it is realised that all men are interdependent and alike the sons of God, the more social Catholic outlook becomes intelligible and sympathetic.

On the strictly religious plane, this change of approach had been shown some time before in the acceptance by many Christian sociologists of Maurice's insistence on the much-neglected fact of the Incarnation. Maurice had been educated among the Friends and Baptists and was interested in the Irvingite church. His salient teaching affirmed that the Incarnation, rather than the Atonement, should be the primary Christian mystery to be considered, as coming first in time; without it the doctrine of the Redemption could not properly be understood. It was said against him that he made light of the Atonement. This is not true; what he did, inferentially, was to criticise that view of it which in his opinion distorted so much Protestant theology.

He asserted as against the Calvinists that Christ was the

Head of every man, and not only of those who believed in Him. Baptism sealed us, rather than made us the children of God. But it was with regard to his doubt as to the everlasting nature of damnation that he strayed most from orthodox belief; he declared that God's mercy would extend beyond the grave. This of course is contrary to Catholic teaching as to Judgment which relies upon the very certain words of our Lord, but was not at all inconsistent with that dislike of belief in the idea of Hell which was rapidly spreading outside the Catholic communion. Seeing that Hell and its torments were the chief subject of Evangelical sermons, the necessity for his breach with them becomes apparent.

For these and similar sentiments, some more and some less orthodox from a Catholic standpoint than the opinions of his fellow clerics, he was deprived of his lectureship at King's College, London, and objections were raised to his appointment to a living. He belonged to no specific party, but he saw, as few did, that the good life on earth, social or individual, was "the assertion of God's order". The Kingdom of God is not a thing to be made by men, it is an act of God, resembling in that respect Creation. His "Socialism" was thus the offspring of his theology and his influence upon later Socialist and socially-minded Christians has been very great.

In the restricted meaning of his relation to the Anglican Church he has been called, erroneously, a broad churchman, but this is quite unimaginative; Maurice, a genius, cannot be placed within any conventional Anglican classification. It is true that he thought that "a person who conscientiously subscribed to the thirty-nine Articles according to his judgment of the grammatical sense is free from any obligation to rule himself by the supposed opinions of others" and he certainly denied the corporate nature of the Church as such, and consequently had little belief in the mystical nature of the Sacraments. Yet he was opposed to any revision of the Prayer Book, and indeed impatient of doctrinal definition. His influence on modern Anglicanism in leading it away from defined dogma cannot be overestimated.

In addition to Kingsley, who still called himself an "old-fashioned high churchman", the immediate influence of Maurice was to be seen in Archdeacon Hare, his brother-in-law, Bishop Thirlwall and F. W. Robertson. The present Christian sociological movement known as "Christendom", of which Canon Widdrington, Professor Demant, Maurice Reckitt, T. S. Eliot the poet, and Dr. Casserly, the sociologist, are leaders, may be said to have derived largely from the teaching of Maurice, both in the theological and social sphere, though it is a strange fact that his followers, unlike their master, have mostly been Anglo-Catholics and have, in varying degree, a firm belief in the necessity for a teaching Church and for the Sacraments.

Apart, however, from the new social approach, an important change was taking place among the Anglo-Catholics who formed the spearhead of the new sociological movement in matters more strictly doctrinal. It is well known how little were the early Tractarians interested in ritual as such, and later, when services became more Catholic, they were justified principally on the grounds that the rubrics of Edward VI's Prayer Books had declared lawful certain practices "until further order be taken". In other words, the early Ritualists based their case on canon or statutory law. Now, however, a different justification is apparent. A more oecumenical attitude was taken. Practices which were universal to the "undivided" Church, as it was termed, for the exclusive claims of Rome were still vehemently opposed, were to be encouraged, whether they had or had not the approval of English lawyers. Thus, of Dr. Darwell Stone, one of the greatest of Anglican theologians of the time, Dr. Cross, his biographer, has written:

"Towards the Church of England, Stone's attitude was different from those of most Tractarians, in that in matters of doctrine and practice his appeal was not to the English formularies, but to an authority wider and more comprehensive. He was convinced that the authority of the

Church of England as such was not more than that of a local and national church. It is only in so far as her teaching is 'the reproduction and re-utterance of what has been universally taught' that it has 'the authority of the Universal church'. He would not have it that the Tractarians were justified in finding in the articles a foundation for their Catholic belief, and here he is fully justified by recent liturgiology and research."

But while Dr. Stone came to these conclusions on grounds of careful study and thought, there were many who were moved by more emotional considerations to "step outside the Prayer Book" and introduce such extra-liturgical services as Devotions before the Blessed Sacrament, Adoration and Benediction. It was to cope with such matters as these that the Royal Commission on Ecclesiastical Discipline was set up in 1904.[1] It reported in 1906 first that "the law of public worship in the Church of England was too narrow for the religious life of the present generation" and also, among other things, that "the machinery for discipline had broken down as the existing courts no longer commanded the respect of the clergy". They also suggested that Letters of Business be sent to the Convocations to consider new rubrics about Vestures, Ornaments and services which "a reasonable recognition of the comprehensiveness of the Church of England seems to demand".

It was from the recommendation of this Commission, admits the present Archbishop of York in his *Church and State in England*, that the process of revision of the Prayer Book started; a very Erastian origin. Not until 1920 was the work of the Convocations concluded, by which time the new National Assembly had come into being, and to them the matter was

[1] The revival of ritualistic practices had been opposed by Sir William Harcourt, particularly from 1898–1900. He denied the right of Bishops to authorise any service outside the Book of Common Prayer. He openly described the Prayer Book as "the Schedule of a Statute", and wrote many letters to *The Times* condemning ritualism. He died before the Commission had reported.

sent—another concession to the laity, for in that Church legislature the non-clerics had a separate legally recognised "House". The most important decision was that the old Prayer Book was to be retained but various optional additions and variations allowed. Had these been merely regulative and undoctrinal no comment would have arisen, but many, more particularly those concerning the Eucharist, were very contentious as they admitted a doctrine of the Communion service, which Protestants in the strict sense had always opposed, and also, most strangely, allowed as alternative the Orthodox rather than the Catholic (and Anglican) view of the nature of consecration of the elements—that is, by the descent upon them of the Holy Spirit (the "Epiklesis"), rather than by the words of our Lord—to be permissible.

Thus, doctrinally, four views of Eucharistic doctrine were now sought to be allowed; the Lutheran and Calvinist of the old Prayer Book, and two new ones, a modified Catholic approach and also the invocation of the Holy Spirit as accepted by the Greeks! No wonder, as Dr. Garbett says, "the Church was divided". That some objected to reservation for the sick, and others claimed that reservation should be without restriction, was perhaps a minor point, though figuring largely at the time. That one Church should permit four doctrines will appear, when the immediate issues have lost their interest, to be more remarkable.

The late Bishop of Gloucester, Dr. Headlam, writing at the time of the 1927 Parliamentary debates, stated, as one of the reasons for revision, that:

"There is a demand made by some that the Prayer Book should be adapted much more to what are called the conditions of modern thought. That is the characteristic of those proposals for revision which were contained in what is called the Grey Book. It means removing everything which conflicts, or seems to conflict, with modern science or criticism, and adapting the prayers and services to the conditions of modern life. The social well-being of the people, the interest of our country, the desire for better international relations, the problem of peace or war, the conflict between capital and labour, and many other similar questions, represent a new outlook and interest. The social and corporate side of Christianity is more prominent than it was." But he wrote also: "It must be emphasized that the adoption of the new Prayer Book lays down principles on which it may be possible for reunion with Nonconformist bodies to become practicable, for it recognises variety in worship. The spiritual freedom and the comprehensiveness of the Church are two necessary conditions for such reunion."

Despite these apologies and admissions, the House of Commons twice threw out the measure primarily on the ground that, in the words of one speaker, "in one generation with the new Prayer Book they could swing all the children of England from the Protestant Reformed Faith to the Roman Catholic Faith". The contrast between this eloquence and the episcopal assurances was bewildering and no one was more bewildered than the ordinary uninstructed lay churchman.

It must not be thought, however, because of all these unedifying differences about ritual and liturgy, that even deeper matters were not in issue. Years before, the publication of *Essays and Reviews* had called forth great anger on account of their suspected heresies. When Temple the elder was about to be appointed Bishop of Exeter (1869), Dr. Pusey protested against the promotion of one of the authors of this "soul-destroying book". From another viewpoint Lord Shaftesbury supported him. The contributions of Jowett, Patterson and H. B. Wilson had argued for more latitude in theology, but Jowett, who was brought before the Vice-Chancellor's court in Oxford, triumphed. Heresy, in a latitudinarian direction no longer gave alarm; in any event the essays were very mild compared with what was to follow thereafter.

The next Symposium which caused an outcry was *Lux Mundi*, which appeared in 1889. The authors who worked in

conjunction were very eminent: Scott Holland, Talbot, Gore
and Moberly. The theory of Evolution is accepted; it was said
to provoke a belief in the "cosmical significance" of the Incarnation "which was a prominent thought in the mediaeval
church". Theology and science move in different planes; one
giving the meaning, the other the method, of Creation. It is
further contended that in experience lies the only proof of the
existence of God—a view which is not in harmony with that
of the Catholic Church and contradicts most of the Scholastics,
St. Thomas and St. Anselm in particular. The view of Maurice
on the Incarnation is upheld, it is said to be the "basis of
dogma". The visible Church and the Sacraments are defended;
the Church is fundamentally Catholic and only incidentally
national.

But it was the article on the Holy Spirit by Dr. Gore, then
Principal of Pusey House, which caused the greatest alarm in
certain circles. It has been said that "the contributors appear
to have been considerably surprised at the great storm with
which its publication was greeted", but the suggestion that
our Lord on becoming Man abandoned some part of His
divine qualities was already very popular on the Continent
among Protestants when Dr. Gore seemed to adopt it to
account for criticisms of the alleged ignorance of Christ of
certain events in the Old Testament. This doctrine of Kenosis
from a Catholic point of view is definite heresy, and the fact
that the author was principal of the Anglo-Catholic Pusey
House shows the gulf which existed between the teaching of
the Catholic Church and that of current Anglo-Catholicism.

It is but fair, however, to say that the Kenotic theory, as
it is called, is no part of official Anglicanism, however many
Churchmen may, in fact, hold it. As Dr. Stone wrote, "That
the Eternal Word itself, even within the sphere of the Incarnation, should be without His divine knowledge is one which
must be rejected." A modified form is expressed by Dr. Cross
that by a process of translation "the human mind would
transmute thought into human knowledge and so make available for our Lord's use in His incarnate mortal life, whatever

it was thus able to receive". However this may be, by 1895 Gore had formulated a view that our Lord on earth was ignorant of certain facts, but that of His own volition He was so ignorant; as he expressed it, "the Incarnation involved a real self-impoverishment, a real self-emptying, a real self-limitation on the part of God".

The avowed aim of the authors was said to be "to put the Catholic Faith into its right relation to modern intellectual and moral problems"—an undertaking subsequently attempted by the authors of another symposium, *Foundations*—but whatever their purpose they certainly did not placate such Anglican theologians as Liddon.

"There is no getting over the fact," he bewailed, "that between Gore's position in the essay in which he denied the verbal inspiration of the Scriptures and Dr. Pusey's teaching on these very subjects, there is nothing short of absolute contradiction."

On the whole, however, there was far less criticism than arose on the publication of *Essays and Addresses*. Whether this was due to the rapid spread of Modernism or indifference it is not easy to say. It will be recalled that the Catholic principle, as laid down by Pope Leo XIII in his encyclical *Providentissimus*, accepts neither the Protestant view of direct verbal inspiration nor that of Gore, for there the Holy Father teaches that God by His supernatural influence so stirred and moved the human writers, and so assisted them, that they rightly conceived in their minds that, and that only, which He bade them write, and that they willed to write it faithfully, and that with unfailing truth they expressed themselves aptly; for otherwise God would not be the author of the whole of the sacred scriptures.

It is convenient here to consider *Foundations*, of which mention has been made, for it is often grouped with *Lux Mundi* as an "accommodating book". It was published in 1912, and endeavours to deal with all the difficulties about the Faith which the authors feel that an educated man might then experience. Its sub-title, "A statement of Christian belief in terms of Modern thought", reveals its purpose.

The chapter on the "modern situation" discloses the vast change which had taken place since the times when rival parties in the Church battled at Oxford within a Christian arena. In 1912, the date of publication, a census was taken of the number of Easter communicants, surely the very minimum of Church worship. In England, of a then population of 36,000,000, the number of practising Anglicans was under two and a half, being little above four per cent in Liverpool and Manchester, to take two representative towns, so that the need to convince the ordinary citizen of the claims of the Anglican Church can never have been greater. The "modern situation", as defined, was instanced in the belief of Bertrand Russell that "nothing can preserve a life beyond the grave and that all the devotion of the ages is destined to extinction in the vast death of the solar system", and even of those more concerned with Faith in that "only the slightness of their theological interest has allowed so many critics to treat the Sermon on the Mount as a purely ethical discourse".

Untaught by an authoritative Church, each of the essayists, like those in *Lux Mundi*, went about the task of restoring belief in his own fashion. We are grown out of the tutelage of "bondage to authority", it is said, and are now in the state of "abstract freedom", which is "the assertion of the right to criticize, and if necessary to deny". The authority of the Church, such as it is in our intermediate state of dependence, must be founded on the corporate experience of saintly men. "The Catholicism of the future," declared Rawlinson, later Bishop of Derby, "cannot disregard the truths of Protestant witness and must to a certain extent reinterpret and revalue (without abandoning) its institutionalism in the light of them."

Another departure from Catholic tradition is disclosed in the philosophic foundations for his creed laid down by W. H. Moberly, who asserts that "the old religion needs a new

K

theology". The traditional basis has broken down, he maintains; a demonstration of the existence of God in the manner of the Schoolmen "has no living influence". Our conception of the universe has changed; "theological systems constructed in an older age have little appeal for the modern mind". The so-called "proofs" are inadequate. We compare this with the assertion of the Vatican Council of 1869 that the existence of God can be proved by the natural reason.

It may be said, in passing, to show the transient view of these opinions, that more recent Anglican theologians, such as Mascall and Farrer, have not scrupled to use the old, here discredited, Thomistic system. "The modern mind" is an unstable criterion of religious truth. For the rest, Canon B. H. Streeter's description of the Gospel account of the Resurrection as a "naive eschatological conception—natural to the men of that day"—to be rejected—and his suggestion that what the disciples saw may have been a subjective vision—is the abandonment not only of Catholic but also of Protestant belief. The Catholic Baron Frederick von Hügel not surprisingly described the essay on the *Being of God* as "wholly unsatisfactory" and Dr. Darwell Stone, though not prepared to protest publicly, declared that "some of its essays suffer from being pervaded with a pragmatist philosophy".

How far this, and similar books, represented the prevailing opinion of Anglicans at the time it is difficult to decide; in any event, as Dr. Cross in his *Darwell Stone* says, the book was

"addressed to a type of modern thought which no longer exists. The Hegelian philosophy of Mr. Moberly made the Christian faith appear more of a *Weltanschaung* than a gospel and its chariness of condemning anything that pretended to be modern meant that the faith expounded lacked drive".

Streeter, in particular, by making it clear that he did not believe in the bodily Resurrection of Christ, "made *Foundations* a byeword".

The Lambeth Conference of Bishops, in 1908, a few years before *Foundations*,[1] had also concerned themselves with the Faith and Modern Thought. The committee on that subject, in a report which was adopted, the burden of which is optimistic, express the belief that

"as a phase of thought, materialism has lost its power, that the thinking mind in man has reasserted the claim to make an existence and value of its own, not expressible in terms of matter since it is only in relation to consciousness that matter as we know it exists".

In so writing the Bishops gave currency to a most unfortunate error, which for a long time confused, and possibly still does confuse, the issue: A belief in the interaction of forces, electrical or other, may be as "materialistic" in the Christian sense as one accepting matter as an ultimate. Belief in an electric basis for the Universe is no more Christian than one which accepts what is crudely called a materialist conception; a view which modern science, in any case, for the moment, has abandoned.

But what is even more unsatisfactory was the demoded assumption of the Bishops that mind is prior to matter; for in all Catholic, and increasingly in non-religious, philosophy, matter and mind are accepted as two complementary aspects of related being.

Since the publication of *Lux Mundi*, however, it must be admitted that the Anglican thinkers have given far more attention to philosophy than was formerly the case. On the whole the Anglo-Catholics have tended to accept Scholasti cism in one form or another as the basis of their systems, while the modernist school have inclined rather to Plato and Plotinus, rejecting the derivatives of Aristotle as too rigid and factual. Unlike the case of the Catholic Church, where, since the time of Leo XIII, the students for the priesthood have been educated in the principles of Thomism, there is no recognised

---

[1] "An effort to break away from the social and theological rigidity of the older Tractarians while retaining their ecclesiastical theory."—HENSON, *Memoirs*.

philosophic school in the Anglican Church. The prevailing scepticism about metaphysic generally has of necessity encouraged a pragmatic and relativist view of theology, which the widespread study of comparative religion has done much to encourage. The older reliance on experience as a religious principle has, to some extent, been given a new life in the existential movement, but, on the whole, it would be true to say that most Anglicans who think philosophically still rely upon Platonic values as their chief justification; declaring the Good, the Beautiful and the True to be of the nature of God and outside the mensurable world of time and space.

In this connection the Gifford lectures of Archbishop Temple deserve careful study. Mr. G. M. Young, a contemporary, speaking of these addresses, comments that "the Aristotelians did not at all approve". And this is not surprising when we remember that Temple in the Gifford lecture, *Nature, Man and God*, had defined the Absolute as a "Commonwealth of Value", the lecturer owing his debt to Caird and the Hegelian Bosanquet.

Nevertheless there are realist elements in his thought; he sees that we must believe that spirit, the ultimate reality, testifies to the reality it informs, but this is a long way from the full acceptance of matter as reality, lasting in the glorified body through eternity, which is Catholic teaching. To Temple, Will rather than Being is the final attribute of God; here he is nearer to Duns Scotus and the mediaeval Franciscans than the Thomists; as Miss Emmet remarks:

"I doubt whether his conversion to 'realism' went very deep. In essence he declines to think of the world as it exists as a rational whole, we must think of it rather as a drama than a picture, as we see it it is strictly unintelligible, for the divine purpose is not yet worked out. We can contribute so far as the Word of God dominates, it is a dynamic process."

Here we see very clearly the influence of Bergson, Whitehead and Alexander. How far Temple's metaphysic still influences

Anglicans today it is not easy to say. Yet it is a great gain that such careful thought should have been presented by him, Professor Taylor and others, for, as Graham Wallace had lamented prophetically in 1914, "The loose anti-intellectualism which now threatens to take the place of the old intellectualism may prove infinitely dangerous." He quotes with sorrow the words of Dr. Robinson to the Church Congress in 1909 that "the function of the intellect is to find reasons for a course of action which, on other than intellectual grounds, we are inclined to desire or approve"; to a Scholastic philosopher, Catholic or Anglican, this is anathema. The fundamental problem, as Dr. Matthews, Dean of St. Paul's, points out in his *Christian Philosophy*, is the place of Revelation in philosophy on which religion so largely depends; he might have added Tradition. From the modernist side, however, he contends that "enlightened religion has now passed beyond that conception of revelation as a rigid and purely external authority".

In this we can no longer listen only to the voice of the Church, for, in the opinion of the Dean of St. Paul's, "We shall not perhaps feel so confident as Newman that we are able to distinguish the true Church from many spurious imitations." Instead he prefers the veridical force, the existence of our "Christian civilisation". This is a phrase often used by European politicians, and when we further read that "the most obvious contrast between Christian civilisation and all others is that it is progressive"—the illustration being that "scientific advance which has revolutionised life and thought during the last hundred years"—the atom bomb had not been made at the time of this writing—one sees how Temple's "dynamic universe" may take many protean shapes. Dr. Matthews, it will be remembered, was for many years Dean of the Theological Faculty of King's College, London, and his opinions are to be taken as equally representative of the Anglican opinion of his time as are those of Dr. Temple.

Finally, to conclude this rapid survey of recent Anglican thought, we note that according to Dr. Thornton (of the Community of the Resurrection), in *Essays Catholic and Critical*, published in 1926, there are two principles of great importance today which illustrate the religious concept of Revelation. There are different grades in the structure of reality; all knowledge is transubjective. As to the first, we have a series: Nature, Man, History and the Incarnation. These four factors in the sequence taken provide all the data we possess for our knowledge of God, so also, to seek the explanation of the world in some simple idea, causation or development was a Victorian over-simplication, derived from Descartes. Today we see that "the Real yields up its secrets only to those who accept it as something given", the dualism of subject and object is in some degree overcome, and Revelation of God is accepted as a " 'giveness' we receive."

Despite these bold attempts to reconcile modern metaphysic, mostly undeistic, with the Christian faith, Professor C. H. Turner probably summed up the general opinion of Anglican philosophers when, in an address to an Anglo-Catholic Congress in 1920, he said: "I trust we may learn from the examples the danger of trying to identify the cause of Christian philosophy with the advocacy of any special doubtful speculative tenets belonging to a philosophical authority, however deservedly famous. The cause of a 'Kantian system' or an 'Hegelian system' is not necessarily the cause of Christ and Christianity," and he inferentially criticized Leo XIII and Benedict XV in their commendation to seminaries of the teaching of St. Thomas when he added:

"I trust the English Church, while always ready to profit by all true thinking, old or new, will never commit itself to an official philosopher. Even if we could afford to be like the Bourbons in never forgetting anything, we dare not be like them in never learning anything. On the day when there is nothing more to be learned in philosophy, philosophy will cease to be anything but a quaint relic of antiquity."

There is little doubt that this eclectic attitude towards the philosophic justification of Faith is one which Anglicans of all opinions will find sympathetic. How far it is sound is a matter which it is not necessary here to discuss.

*   *   *   *   *

When we pass from problems of philosophy to those of social justice we find ourselves at once in a more resolute, less hesitant, atmosphere. Here, if anywhere, the Anglo-Catholics, for they were the pioneers in this field, have every reason to congratulate themselves. In two generations they have converted the better part of the Anglican Church from a grudging acceptance of its responsibilities to a very real concern for the future of society. As the Fabians permeated the trade union and Labour movements of their times with their collectivist ideas, so in the Church of England a small group of very able men, without specific organisation, but of a like mind, gradually built up the conception of a society which would be ordered on Christian lines so far as the sinfulness of man would permit, being neither exclusively individualistic nor socialistic, but establishing a general "welfare state" while having regard always to the sanctity of personality. On the question of the family, unlike many reformers, they stood foursquare with their Catholic allies—for in this field, as *Copec* and the later *Sword of the Spirit* movements showed, doctrinal differences presented no direct difficulty. They favoured the corporate action in industry of self-government in forms approximating to the old guild system and ventured to criticise the plutocratic use of credit in the interests of high finance. That this outlook is now familiar to many Anglicans is due in large measure to the work, in speaking and writing, of this little League of the Kingdom of God, later to be known as the "Christendom group". Their chief books were *The Return of Christendom* (1922) and a quarter of a century later *The Prospects of Christendom*, which were largely read, the former having a preface by Bishop Gore.[1] Their work ran

[1] And an epilogue by G. K. Chesterton, his last Anglican contribution.

parallel to that of the Catholic Social Guild, which had been inspired by the encyclicals *Rerum Novarum* and *Quadragesimo Anno*.

In this work, Gore, Scott Holland, and later Temple, even when Archbishop of Canterbury, gave wise leadership. The actual protagonists in the field—they deserve mention—were Canon Widdrington, and his fellow clerics Peck, Casserly and Demant, and among laymen, Penty, Reckitt and, both as Anglican and Catholic, the great genius G. K. Chesterton.

In a publication of the Anglo-Catholic Church Union called *A Christian Realm*, the opinions of these Anglican sociologists are thus admirably summarised:

"The world was designed by God to be the scene of a divine order. The failure of mankind, initiated at the Fall, recurrent in every moment of man's sin, frustrates that intention; it does not change it. The Catholic Faith insists that man, though fallen, is not totally depraved. The life of man, created by God, redeemed by Christ, succoured at every moment by the grace of God, is still the sphere in which God's Kingdom may come and His will be done, in earth as it is in heaven. Because of this, the Church has a right and duty to criticise and to speak upon the ordering of human society.

It is a fundamental Christian doctrine that there is a natural order of human life, laid down by God, made known to conscience and illuminated by revelation, by which all human societies must be judged according to their tendency to conform to it, though conformity is never fully attained. Such an order in proportion as it was realised would really be Order as opposed to Anarchy, because therein human purposes would be seen in due proportion, and men would therefore stand in right relation not only to one another, but to nature and to the earth, which would be honoured and served, instead of being neglected and robbed. The impulse towards the establishment of such an order, no less than its basic principles, is derived from God's laws implicit in His creation, not from mere human altruism nor from secular moral aspiration. Thus to identify this order with the idea of a natural law is not to imply that the attempt to conform to it could succeed without God's grace. The grace of God is needed, both by those who can recognise it as divinely given and by those who cannot, as a means not only of attaining to the elements of such an order but also of preserving them. A natural order would not be a Utopia without sin. But it would be a society in which sin could be distinguished for what it was, not disguised as necessity, hallowed as 'enterprise', or revered as progress. Man in such an order might choose wrong, but he would be free to choose and would know what he was choosing."

Perhaps the most cogent evidence of the growth of interest in social questions is afforded by a comparison of the ineffectual early reports of the Lambeth Conferences of Bishops with later pronouncements. It does not appear that, until 1897, industrial problems figured prominently on the agenda, though the Conferences had been held since 1867. Then at length they stress the brotherhood of man and in the 1897 report encourage co-operation. In 1924, largely on the initiative of Dr. William Temple, a great Conference was held on Christian politics, economics and citizenship (*Copec*). It followed a report at the Lambeth Conference of Bishops in 1908 at which resolutions on *The Moral Witness of the Church* in relation to social and economic questions were presented. There the moral obligations of the worker, owner and consumer were all emphasised; but also, what is very significant, as illustrating a departure from the extreme individualism of former days, it is said:

"The law must help. Hardly anyone can be found to advocate a return to the *laissez-faire* of the days preceding the Factory Acts. Here, then, is a new department of duty.

The individual Christian is also a citizen. As a citizen he must inform himself on economic questions and take his share of public service."

In affirming this, the Conference in effect endorsed the report of the Canterbury Convocation on the *Moral Witness of the Church* on economic subjects. In 1920 the Lambeth Conference went so far as to say, "Since the beginning of the industrial revolution only a minority of members of our Church have interested themselves in the social application of the Gospel." They assert that "now the conscience of the Christian Community has been stirred".[1]

An opportunity to manifest this new interest soon appeared. The great coal dispute of 1925, followed by the General Strike, 1926, induced certain of the Anglican Bishops, including Dr. Temple, then Bishop of Manchester, the Bishop of Lichfield, the Bishop of Winchester and others to speak and make reports urging specific means of settlement. For this activity they were much attacked, but while, to quote Dr. Iremonger in his *Life of Archbishop William Temple*,

"by organised labour organised religion had hitherto been held to embody the reactionary spirit of a privileged caste and to be consistently opposed to the welfare and progress of the workers, notable leaders of the Churches had now come into the open with an independent and unprejudiced outlook."

[1] In the Bishop of Winchester's preface to the Report of the two archbishops on *Christianity and Industrial Problems* (1919) he speaks of the necessity of repentance for the "undue subservience of the Church to the possessing, employing and governing classes of the past". After referring to Christ as the Great Emancipator, the Report remembers with shame how "Christians" retarded the emancipation of the negro slave, conveniently ignoring that in Christ there is neither bond nor free; it then mentions the liberating work of Wilberforce and Clarkson, but goes on to suggest that there are forms of slavery and semi-slavery existing in our midst today. "A future age will probably look upon some features of our industrial system with something of the same feelings which are aroused in us when we survey the nineteen centuries which it has taken to make a professedly Christian world apply Christian principles to the case of slavery."

Next followed, after the outbreak of the Second World War, a conference suggested by the Industrial Christian Fellowship, at which again Dr. Temple, then Archbishop of York, presided. This time it was confined to Anglicans, its object stated to be to consider from an Anglican view

> "what are the fundamental facts which are directly relevant to the ordering of the new society that is quite evidently emerging, and how Christian thought can be shaped to play a leading part in the reconstruction after the war is over."

The speakers included T. S. Eliot, Dorothy Sayers, Sir Richard Acland, Kenneth Richmond, Dr. Demant and Mr. Maurice Reckitt, whose paper was read. The chief issue, raised by Sir Richard Acland, was the socialist one that "common ownership" is a fundamental Christian principle. It was a view which had previously been rejected at Lambeth Conferences in 1888 and 1908 and by several papal encyclicals. In the end, however, it was agreed that it may be a stumbling block making it harder for men to live Christian lives "for the ultimate ownership of the principal resources of the community to be vested in private owners". Since that time collective legislation has made this subject of somewhat less importance. The substance of the conclusions of this Malvern Conference appeared in a volume issued by the Christendom group, led by Dr. Demant and Maurice Reckitt, who were, with the Archbishop, not pledged to specific socialist solutions, in a symposium called *The Prospect for Christendom*, and in 1942 Temple's *Christianity and the Social Order* to the same effect appeared in the popular Penguin series and sold nearly 150,000 copies.

At the same time, while not denying the effect of these and other appeals to the social conscience, it would be an error to suppose that the whole Anglican Church was converted to some form of what used to be called Christian Socialism. The Church of England continued for the most part to be a governing and middle-class institution; in fact, by 1940, it may be said that the Anglican community, so far as its effective government was concerned, was still almost entirely composed of the comparatively affluent. The appeal by Missions and the like to the masses in the towns, though calling for great self-sacrifice on the part of the missioners, numerically was insignificant. A communicating congregation of 400 in an industrial parish of some 20,000 was deemed a great achievement. Among the "enlightened" classes, the attempts made by Lambeth Conferences and other meetings "to reconcile the Faith and the modern mind", to quote the prevailing ecclesiastical phrase, failed with the great majority. The sceptical outlook of philosophers such as Bertrand Russell was far more persuasive, for even the older Idealism, derived from Hegel, from Green, Bosanquet and their school, had perished at the Universities. The materialism of the Communists may have been considered crude, but chiefly, and this fact is often missed, because it was too dogmatic. The optimism expressed as late as 1908 at the Lambeth Conference that "the dominance of materialism as a spiritual power had now been notably checked" was shown to have no foundation. Indeed it is now evident that a vitalistic view of the Universe may as readily support some form of pantheism or emergent deity, such as Wells envisaged, and be as entirely non-Christian as may what has been called Materialism.

Another obstacle in the way of those who would give to the Anglican communion a social conscience was the incapacity, arising necessarily and probably wisely from their outlook, of the Christendom group and their allies to take any active part in party politics, since each, whether Conservative, Labour or Liberal, represented a secular dogma which the social Christians could, at most, regard as no more than an expedient. As Maurice Reckitt has written in his *Christian in Politics*:

"It is easy to say that it is a moral duty for the Christian to accept his obligations as a citizen, and do his best to fulfil them in national and local politics. Just because religion has lost so much of its influence over the minds of those who claim to direct the currents of the modern world, the political issues of today have largely lost contact with essential realities. There is something missing in our politics today."

This view, inevitably, denies to its holders much of the machinery of publicity, in Parliament, in the press, and even on the broadcaster, which, in our complex mass society, has become so essential if people are to be acquainted with any specific opinions. In truth there is danger that essentially Christian conceptions such as vocation, personality and freedom of will and expression will be forgotten at a time when collective forms of social justice, unmoved by Christian considerations, are being accepted by the modern world. The failure of the Christendom group to maintain their organ *Christendom* and their weekly *New Witness* is an indication that, apart from their own circle, the nation, as a whole, is even less ready today to listen to the Christian sociologists than it was at the time of *Copec*. It will be noticed that, save for the specific Malvern Conference, none of these social activities and thought in the application of the Faith to society was peculiarly Anglican. Broadly speaking, it may be said that those elements which emphasised the Incarnation and the Kingdom of God on earth were sympathetic to the idea of a visible Church, and the acceptance by the Anglo-Catholic Church Union of a sociological department and summer school disclosed a change in their attitude towards economic questions very different from the days of the old English Church Union. The biography of Lord Halifax, for example, the Anglo-Catholic lay leader, shows little or no awareness on his part of social problems.

Morever, within the accommodating Church of England, there still remains a core of Evangelicals, now strengthened by the influence of the neo-Protestantism of Barth, Brunner and others of the "Crisis" school. By temperament and theology these low churchmen were concerned more for the salvation of the individual soul, almost atomically considered, and in his redemption, and many still regarded commerce and the pursuit of gain as the chief rightful secular activity of man. To them the whole notion of the Kingdom on earth makes little appeal or is considered almost irrelevant. From the beginning they looked upon the movements for secular economic justice with suspicion, if not with alarm, but they are a decreasing number. From an Anglican point of view the far greater danger was that even the best of social reformers would make their appeal to the people on grounds wholly secular, and this is in fact what has happened.

In the post-war organisation, the fundamentally Catholic *Sword of the Spirit*, an attempt was made to gather all those who are concerned not only for social justice, but also for its development on Christian lines, in one undenominational effort. The basis of the *Sword* was the recognition of the Natural Law, a not surprising fact in so far as its direction and inspiration came principally from Catholics. The present Archbishop of Canterbury, then Bishop of London, was moved to speak of it as "a measure of joint action such as has not happened since the Reformation". *The Religion and Life* movement of the Anglicans and Free Churches for some time acted with the *Sword of the Spirit*, and many of the former doubtless first learned of the social theology of the Catholic Church as it had developed since the days of St. Thomas Aquinas from these contacts. To quote Dr. Iremonger, "Anglican theologians might be encouraged to undertake some joint study of the Natural Law as the basis of Christian living." Nevertheless, it must be admitted, the average Anglican clergyman still knows little more of natural law (or natural theology) than did his predecessors.

However all this may have been, the introduction of the "Welfare state", and the nationalisation of most of the basic industries after the war, have produced an entirely new situation. The attention of Christian reformers has been diverted rather to the absence of the vocational responsibility of the workers in the new state industries, the fears of over-direction in the provision of benefits and the restriction of the right to strike evidenced in regulations. A fear of Belloc's "Servile State" has largely replaced the condemnation of a plutocratic one, for though wealth has been more evenly distributed than the early Christian socialists ever thought possible, it is freedom rather than subsistence which is now threatened. The futile employment of leisure and the growth of social and individual amorality are also subjects of disquiet. The present modern Christian sociologist faces a world very different from that of his predecessors.

It can scarcely be denied that the ending of the first Great War found the Church of England, for want of any authoritative guidance, in a state of deplorable confusion. In matters sociological, in which, as we have seen, no peculiarly Anglican principles were involved, the Church maintained a more or less coherent policy of enlightenment, and so also in some, though by no means all, cognate moral issues,[1] but when it is asked what did the Anglican Church, as such, teach in 1945, it is impossible to give any exact answer. The elasticity and liberality of mind on which it had so often congratulated itself had brought its Nemesis, and in a general permission to its members to think whatsoever they pleased, provided it was not definitely anti-Christian, the result had come about that the majority of its members had ceased to think at all, or rather ceased to think to such an extent as to produce any reliable conclusions. That discipline had broken down was a constant cry, but discipline needs an order and standard to which obedience must be given, and the only discoverable one, that derived from the Thirty-Nine Articles, the Prayer Book and the Acts of Uniformity had long since ceased to have operative force as a living tradition.

Confronted with this situation, it had been the hope of some Anglicans, expressed under the leadership of William Temple in the *Life and Liberty* movement, following a

---

[1] On such matters as Divorce, and other problems of sex, the Anglicans are by no means in agreement.

National Mission, that if the Church were left to legislate for herself, subject of course to the overriding veto of Parliament, that much reform might be effected. The self-government desired was one which would include the laity, and the Establishment would continue. A report of the committee of the Archbishops on *Church and State* ". . . to enquire what changes are advisable in order to secure in the relations of Church and State a fuller expression of the spiritual independence of the Church as well as of the national recognition of religion" was published in 1916. It declared that by the time of the Reformation "Rome had done its work and the time had come for National Churches" and that under a National Church the "Liturgy and public services of the Church have from 1549 to the present time been prescribed by successive Acts of Uniformity (1549, 1552, 1559, 1661, 1870). The existing Prayer Book was prepared by Convocation and was not altered by Parliament," and that "The thirty-nine Articles of Religion published by Convocation in 1563 with the Queen's authority, subscription to which by the clergy was made obligatory by Act of Parliament in 1571, constitute, together with the Prayer Book, the formal statement of the Church of England's teaching as recognised by the State."

Morever it is asserted that "in all these changes the Crown had the body of the nation at its side, and it was emphatically a work through and with the laity".

Later, after 1689, "the direct intervention of the sovereign in Church affairs largely disappeared. The personal monarchy giving way to 'constitutional' government, Parliament became the heir to much of the royal supremacy. It might seem that this would mean the community entering into more open control of its own Church, with a consequent increase in the functions of the laity. But it was not so. The changes which 'toleration' produced, especially in Parliament itself, had a precisely opposite result. The direct influence of the Church laity upon the government of Church affairs was minimised almost to the point of obliteration." This they deplore, and in their findings recommend what in effect became the National

Assembly with its constituent diocesan and parochial councils. To achieve this a national agitation was set on foot, the *Life and Liberty* movement, and eventually the "Enabling Bill" became law. The number of laymen and clerics in the Assembly is about equal, for it is conceded that the laity are to be effectually consulted about ecclesiastical legislation, and the electors are all baptised persons who declare "they are members of the Church of England and do not belong to any other religious body not in communion with it". The extreme breadth of this franchise, it is said, caused Bishop Gore to resign his see by way of protest. The membership of the Councils is expressly restricted to Communicants, so by inference electors need not necessarily be Communicants at all. In reality the electoral roll is small.

The relation of this mixed assembly to Convocation is not at all clear; we have seen how they were consulted about the revision of the Prayer Book. In any event the Assembly has brought into the Church of England an element of congregational control which is not at all unpopular though entirely uncatholic, and the many disputes which have arisen between parochial church councils and their incumbents (the parochial councils must now be consulted before appointment is made), together with a spate of legislation of a disciplinary kind, has much diminished the former independence of incumbents. The Reformation, as has been written by the Archbishop of York, was a lay movement and Parliament at one time an assembly of lay churchmen, so that the influence of the Assembly in the long run is likely to be in a Protestant rather than a Catholic direction. For the Catholic Church is governed by authority from above, as it was in the times of the Apostles, and no instructed Catholic wishes to comply in Church matters with modern secular aspirations to be "democratic". On the other hand, the insistence on membership of the Church of England, while, as Dr. Henson said, "sectarianising" the Church, does at least confine its franchise to baptised persons who are not prepared to deny their membership. Parliament, however, which need not even be predominantly

Christian, having still the last word in its refusal to resolve that any measure be presented for the royal assent, is still supreme, nor has it lost the power directly to legislate on Church affairs.

Armed with the power of the National Assembly the Bishops, following, as has been noted, the advice of a secular Royal Commission, decided to attempt to restore their broken authority by themselves amending the Prayer Book. The work had been undertaken before the period of which we now write, and its legislative failure was very recent, so that the situation which confronted the Anglican Church at the beginning of its fifth centenary epoch falls within the ambit of our present consideration. Although the proposed new book contained a number of minor alterations which need not detain us, the real purpose was, as Dr. Headlam, the Bishop of Gloucester, frankly wrote,

"that we should have a Prayer Book which legalizes the many and various changes which have been gradually made in the custom and use of the Church, which allows a reasonable variety in many directions, which permits many things to be done, which are widely desired and are clearly not inconsistent with the traditions of the Church of England, and will therefore enable those who have to administer the law of the Church to forbid definitely what is, in the opinion of the great majority of members of the Church, inconsistent with Anglican tradition."

But what *is* the "Anglican tradition"? According to the Thirty-Nine Articles it is a mixture of Lutheran and Calvinist doctrine; the Anglo-Catholics, on the other hand, would read into it the whole or part of the old Catholic faith, excluding the authority of the See of Rome, some going as far as Henry VIII in his *King's Book*. Another group would still regard the Anglican Church as the "nation at prayer", regardless of the fact that the great majority of the citizens are no longer practising or even nominal members, and some would have it so comprehensive as to permit denial of the physical resurrection of our Lord or the Virgin Birth; all these and other schools claim the Tradition, and the Bishops' conferences at Lambeth, while dealing in detail with immediate problems, have, on the whole, carefully abstained from defining their specific interpretation of the traditional Christian faith, probably because if they attempted the task they would have to confess a disastrous disagreement.

We are by now accustomed to a British Commonwealth which includes nations not under allegiance to the King, though formerly it had universally been maintained that allegiance was the essential element which bound the Empire together, but in matters spiritual it is doubtful whether this pragmatic manner of dealing with conflicting claims is possible or appropriate.

Nor must it be thought that all Anglo-Catholics favoured an alternative rite which permitted under regulation reservation of the Sacrament for the use of the sick, but not for devotions or adoration. Dr. Darwell Stone and a number of others who desired the restoration of full Catholic practice and ceremonial saw in the measure proposed to Parliament by the National Assembly merely a device to achieve a discipline and new restriction which they could not accept.

The result was remarkable. Not only did it show to those promoters of the National Assembly, the "Life and Liberty movement", that Parliament still controlled the manner of their prayers and official beliefs, but also it placed the Bishops in an impossible position, for how could they, without the deepest humiliation, oppose the clergy for doing that which they, Convocation and the Assembly had all held to be legitimate? It looked as if the long-expected crisis had come. Even the erstwhile Erastian and modernist Dr. Henson, the Bishop of Durham, was converted to disestablishment as the only solution. As Dr. Garbett has written, "The Church had been subject to open humiliation." In the end the Bishops issued a declaration, asserting the right of the Church to formulate its own faith in worship, and later, with the approval of the Lower Houses of Convocation, the Bishops resolved that they would "be guided by the proposals set forth in the Book of 1928 and would endeavour to secure that the practices which were consistent neither with the Book of 1662 nor with the Book of 1928 shall cease".

This decision annoyed not only the Protestants but also the Erastians. The Dean of the Arches, Sir Lewis Dibdin, spoke of the Bishops disregarding the House of Commons; he pointed out that, notwithstanding the Enabling Act by which measures might be presented to Parliament for the royal approval, "the power of Parliament was intended to remain unaltered and absolute".

It is the habit of Anglican Bishops and clergy, one cannot escape their phrase, to make claim to an "enriched" Order of Communion, but, with every respect to the users of this and similar expressions, they evade the real question. Creed and doctrine should precede Liturgy, which is but an overt expression of belief. This is why the Articles of Religion, despite attempts to belittle them, must still be more authoritative than inferences drawn from the words of the Liturgy. Until the content of belief is decided, and in the Church of England it never has been (and for want of belief in a divinely appointed authority probably never can be) these disputes about ornaments, clothing and furniture must appear to the onlooker as somewhat vain.

"The Church at home requires freedom to bring its public worship more into relation with the thought and understanding of the people of today," says Dr. Garbett; it is the old error of *Lux Mundi* and *Foundations*, so wittily expressed by Mgr. Knox, "Not is it true, but can I get Jones to see it in that light?" In the event the Anglo-Catholic clergy as a whole continued their "illegalities" and the Modernists to write and preach heresy. Meanwhile the number of the priesthood grew less; in 1930 there were 16,750 clergy engaged in the Anglican Church, today, with an increased population, probably fewer than 14,000. In the last pre-war years there were 590 ordinations, in the first two years since the Second World War,

183. It is little consolation to Anglicans to know that the number of active communicants has probably fallen away proportionately.[1]

In the face of this increasing impotence, the only remedy seemed to some Anglicans to lie in union with other Christian bodies. Not that the promoters of such a device, though it would have horrified the Anglicans of earlier ages, are consciously insincere. The feeling that our Lord intended His Church to be one was never lost, but the fact that such a Church already existed and had, since the first Pentecost, been founded on St. Peter and his successors is still, though with decreasing fervour, rejected.

Thus in 1878, at the Lambeth Conference, there being 100 Anglican Bishops present, among other things it was resolved that "The fact that a solemn protest is raised in so many churches and Christian communities throughout the world against the usurpations of the See of Rome and against the novel doctrines promulgated by its authority is a subject of thankfulness to Almighty God." In 1888 the Conference, while asserting as an "essential article" the "Historic Episcopate", asked for "brotherly conference with the representatives of other Christian communions in the English-speaking races". The nationalistic basis of the proposed unity, one not necessarily of belief, will be noted. Hasty and ill-considered steps towards closer relations with the Eastern Orthodox, while hoping for "friendly ones", are deprecated. Of Rome nothing is said. In 1897, more references to the "usurped authority of the Church of Rome" appear and "the grave and earnest men of France, Italy, Spain and Portugal who have been driven to

[1] According to the Rector of Chislehurst, to maintain the ratio of 1914 the increased population would require some 30,000 priests, whereas there are now 13,680; and of these, as is well known, an important percentage consists of men dying in harness, through sickness or old age, who are unable to retire. It may well be that the really effective force is considerably lower. If so, allowing the Bishop's figure of annual loss of 550 each year by death or retirement, the necessary intake for each of the next ten years might well approach 2000, as against the 460 recommended for training last year. Since it takes five years to train a priest, this would give us by 1966 the resumption of the 1914 ratio, which in those days was held to be grievously insufficient.

free themselves from the burden of unlawful terms of communion imposed by the Church of Rome" are congratulated.
Again approaches are made to the Eastern Orthodox and its
chief authorities, and this regardless of the fact that the only
possible agreement which the Orthodox could reach would be
with the Anglo-Catholics, for they alone of Anglicans hold
without qualification the doctrine of the visible Church of
which they contend they are divinely appointed members,
and hold in part the doctrine of the sacrifice of the Mass and
other "illegal" doctrines which were repudiated in one form
or another in England in the reign of Elizabeth and have
never been restored. One is tempted to say that the only basis
of such orthodox reunion would be a common fear and hatred
of Rome. As was said:

> "it is recognised that any proposal for unity with the
> 'Roman Church' would be entertained by the authorities
> of that Church only on condition of absolute submission
> and the acceptance of those errors, both in doctrine and in
> worship against which in faithfulness of God's holy word
> and to the true principles of His Church, we have for three
> centuries been bound to protest."

As to alliance with the Presbyterian and non-episcopal
churches, in 1888, to the Scriptures, Apostles and Nicene
Creed and the two Protestant sacraments, as conditions of
reunion, was added the "Historic Episcopate". This insistence
on Episcopacy so far has proved an intractable obstacle,
although it had been in part waived in the case of the Bishop
of Jerusalem, whereby Prussian ministers who held the
Lutheran Augsburg Confession and signed the Thirty-Nine
Articles were to be ordained by the Archbishop of Canterbury.
In 1919, however, a proposal for union between the
Anglicans in India and some non-episcopal congregations was
seriously supported, not, as in the case of Jerusalem, by politicians, but by Bishops and clerics of the Anglican Church
itself. In 1930 a report was presented to the Lambeth Congress

on the matter. There had been held at Lausanne in 1927 a World Conference on *Faith and Order* which considered the nature of the Church, the Creed, the Doctrine of the Sacrament and the Christian ministry, and on the principles there contained the South Indian scheme was considered. At that time it was but an outline. It was objected by Lord Quickswood that the scheme offered no "security of orthodoxy", and by others that it depreciated the importance of Episcopacy, and generally on traditional grounds by the Church Union. Nevertheless, in 1945, the General Council of the Churches of India, Burma and Ceylon accepted the scheme as finally drafted. The four dioceses of South India directly concerned agreed to a severance for the time being from the Anglican communion and in September 1947 the new Church was created, the Lambeth Conference of 1930 having expressed "their strong desire that the venture should be made and the union inaugurated", but it was later admitted at the 1948 Conference that "the scheme as finally adopted is in certain ways less satisfactory to Anglicans than the scheme the 1930 Conference had before it"—the alterations having "given serious ground for anxiety". Now, as finally constituted, the Church consists of ex-Anglicans, members who are not Anglican and have never been ordained episcopally, and those ordained since the union. The Bishops were divided whether this semi-Anglican body was or was not a living part of the one Holy, Catholic and Apostolic Church, and there the matter rests.

The movement towards reunion with Dissenters was not confined to India or Ceylon. The 1920 appeal from Lambeth to the Free Churches in England resulted in a conference with them. But, as the Archbishop, Dr. Lang, had to admit of some of them, "they have no real care about a visible church at all. I am afraid they are still content if only they can preach at St. Paul's and communicate at our altars". They raised the point why should they be ordained if already in "real ministries of Christ's word and sacraments in the universal church". It was proposed by the Anglicans that they should be "authorised" by a Bishop or conditionally ordained. The

proposals failed, but they go to show how far responsible
Anglicans had travelled in a liberal direction since the days of
the Oxford Movement. The proposal that "ministers not
episcopally ordained, who were working towards the idea of
union, should occasionally be authorised to preach in Anglican
churches, and that non-Anglicans might, in certain circumstances, be admitted to Communion" discloses a latitude in
Anglican practice which, in the absence of any ultimate criteria
of orthodoxy, is likely to increase with the passage of time.
Indeed already in 1930 two Unitarians, Dr. Jacks and Mr.
Redfern, had preached in Liverpool Cathedral. In the result, it
is true, the Upper House of Convocation at York, referring to
the discretion vested in a Bishop, agreed in 1922 to invite
preachers, not Anglicans, at special services, but declared that
this should not extend to persons who were not Trinitarians.

The persistent inability of the Anglican hierarchy to understand the Catholic attitude to schismatic or separated bodies of
Christians is astonishing, seeing that the Catholic Church has
never failed to emphasise the fact that she alone is the mystical
body of Christ, outside of which there is no other church. Yet
when the Anglican Bishops spoke in 1930 of the failure of
attempts at reunion with the Catholic Church, they refer to the
abortive efforts of Lord Halifax on two occasions, in 1896,
when Pope Leo XIII condemned Anglican Orders, and at
Malines from 1921 to 1925. On these they comment, "We
would therefore greatly value further elucidation from the
Roman Catholic side on the matter of such co-operation, and
would be thankful if the way could be found to make it fully
effective." The earlier denunciations of Rome have disappeared,
no more is heard of "errors" and "usurped authority". That
Rome refused to send a representative to the World Conference
of Christians at Amsterdam appears to some Anglicans surprising; it is amazing, after so many years of explanation of the
Catholic position, that those not in her communion, however
sympathetic or hostile, fail to grasp the divine uniqueness which
the Catholic Church claims for herself, to last until the end of
time. As has been said by a prominent Dominican:

"It becomes more and more difficult to find words to convey the reality. If we abandon the word 'intolerant' in relation to truth, we are still left with the fact that the Church cannot compromise in any doctrine. In matters of dogma she cannot meet people half-way and agree to only a partial acceptance of her teaching. The faith is unique and all of a piece; and so it is impossible for it to exist with a denial of any single point in the body of doctrines. To take a pertinent example: it is frequently reiterated that the fundamental principles of the Anglican Church contain the right and the duty of private judgment and the ultimate appeal to Scripture as the Word of God. The Archbishop of Canterbury re-emphasised both these points in his widely publicised articles on *The Beliefs of the Church of England*. Bishop Carey, celebrating the memory of Dean Church, gives four essential principles as the foundation of the Church of England: (a) *The Bible* the final reference, (b) *Creeds* as summaries of the Word, (c) *The Apostolic Succession* in the Ministry, (d) *The Sacraments*. Now these teachings are indeed characteristic of Protestantism, and they are no doubt the Protestant tenets which Lambeth hoped to unite with Catholic beliefs in the broad unity of the Church of England. But in fact the Catholic teaching cannot co-exist with the principles of private judgment and the supremacy of the Bible. The Church says it is one or the other, as indeed Karl Barth has asserted on behalf of his own point of view. There is no suggestion of compulsion or forcible suppression of error, but the power of truth is itself compelling. Surely an occasional impatient gesture on the part of a Catholic is understandable when he is asked to plunge again and again into elaborate arguments from history, when he is asked to reconsider the question of Anglican Orders and so on. All this is so irrelevant, when the question is one of error which must be rejected. The Catholic may seem intolerant in an evil sense; but this may be simply natural impatience derived from original sin. And the same applies to the toleration claimed for the

propagation of untruth. It is only a drunken Catholic who
will break up a Salvation Army meeting; it is, nevertheless,
an indifferent Catholic who will pass the meeting by with
the thought that it is simply 'good religion'. Men are still
upset by an untruth even when it is not a deliberate untruth. A father who 'tolerates' fibs among his children is
not regarded as a good parent. And similarly a good and
zealous Catholic cannot 'tolerate' what is inimical to the
truth which he holds from God."

The definition by the Pope of the Assumption of the
Blessed Virgin, a doctrine held by Catholics, by the Easterns
and by the Church in England before the Reformation, called
forth vehement protests from certain Anglicans, ostensibly
because the decree would make reunion with Rome more
difficult; in 1854, on the definition of the Immaculate Conception, that objection was not raised; indeed in those days
a dogma which it was supposed would make it the more
difficult for Anglicans to join the Catholic Church was in
many circles a matter of congratulation. In any case it must be
clear to the unprejudiced observer that any union other than
submission to the Holy See (which in the case of submission
to Cardinal Pole as papal legate was national and corporate)
must, if Catholicism be rightly understood, be impossible.

There remains, however, the question of a reunion of
Protestants, a project far more probable of success, and, in
theory, offering far less difficulties. A recent evangelical
conference expressed the view that

"Increased unity between the Church of England and
the Free Churches would greatly strengthen co-operation
between Church and State at the present time. It is, therefore, the duty of the national Church and of all its members
to do all in their power to promote reunion with other
Protestant Churches."

A more official report suggests that

"authority in the Church of England should formally sanction the extension to ministers of the Church of Scotland, of invitations to preach in the parish churches in England, and, similarly, formal approval should be given to the acceptance by ministers of the Church of England of invitations to preach in parish churches in Scotland.

The conference also suggests that authority in the Church of England should formally sanction the admission of baptised communicant members of the Church of Scotland, cut off by distance from convenience of access to the ministrations of their own Church, or, in special personal circumstances, to Holy Communion in the Church of England.

The report states that the converse proposal regarding extension to communicants of the Church of England out of reach when in Scotland of access to Episcopalian ministrations occasioned greater difficulty. The joint conference decided not to make any recommendation with regard to this matter.

The report on Church Union in Ceylon proposes that the new Church of Lanka (the Sinhalese name for Ceylon) should include the Methodist, Presbyterian, and Baptist Churches in Ceylon, as well as the present Anglican diocese of Colombo and the diocese of Kurunagala in the South India Church scheme. It would not form part of the Anglican Communion."

In the eyes of Anglicans, apart from the question of the royal supremacy, there remains only the problem of Episcopacy, the fourth limb of the "Lambeth Quadrilateral". How is this to be overcome? Clearly a closer study of the office of Bishop is needed to decide whether it is or is not of the essence of the Anglican Church, before a judgment is reached from a dissenting or Anglican angle. We find that as time passed, after the Church of England was established, the belief in the divine nature of Episcopacy grew weaker. It is a remarkable fact that until the eighteenth century few Anglican theologians disputed the doctrine of the apostolical succession, their claim for the catholicity of the Church of England was largely based upon it. Thus Jewel in 1567 speaks of his "predecessors the Catholic Bishops", adding "we succeed them in place", and in the preface to the Ordinal, written by Cranmer in 1552, it is said, speaking of Bishops (and priests), "from the apostles time there hath been these orders of Ministers in Christ's Church", and, again to quote Jewel, "our Bishops are made in form and order as they have been ever". Whitgift also declared that the "episcopal degree is an institution apostolical and divine". Bancroft asserts the Episcopacy to be apostolic while Bilson traces it back even to the Old Testament; he calls it the apostolical delegation. Hooker wrote to the effect that "a thousand five hundred years and upward the Church of Christ hath now continued under the sacred regiment of Bishops", while Overall agrees with Bilson in giving an Old Testament ancestry for the episcopal state. Later we find Sanderson arguing the Bishops to be of "apostolical institution and approbation". "The episcopacy is an ancient, holy and divine institution," maintains Laud. That there were less positive opinions, like that of Chillingworth, who however stated that "episcopal government is acknowledged to have been universally received in the Church presently after the apostles times", will be admitted, but this is far from denying the apostolical succession, and Bramhall, who allows that Episcopacy was universally received without opposition, commented that from the days of the apostles till the year of Christ 1500 there was not one poor village that was governed without a Bishop. Without putting the claim as high as the earlier divines, he yet accepts Episcopacy as a necessary part of the Anglican constitution. Cosin also takes a moderate view, declaring that "the power of ordination was restrained to Bishops rather by apostolical practice and the perpetual custom and canons of the Church than by any absolute precept that Christ or His apostles gave about it".

The coming of the Calvinist, William III and a general Whig sympathy with Nonconformists had the effect of discountenancing all such exalted episcopal claims, while the surrender of their dioceses by the Non-Jurors and the installation of Whig Bishops tended in the same direction. Tillotson, who became Archbishop of Canterbury, would have allowed Presbyterians to serve as ministers without specific ordination on mere imposition of hands from a Bishop, a device which the Church of England may yet adopt, and proposals to the like effect were drafted by commissioners for the purpose, but without result. There is little doubt that if William had had his way, the Church of England on the Elizabethan model as such would have ceased to exist and become merged in a general Protestant body, the Bishops, as Burnet desired, remaining with a reduced status as in Lutheran Germany. There were, of course, upholders of the more ancient tradition, such as Beveridge and Stillingfleet, and during the reign of Anne the apostolical doctrines once again found favour. Hoadly, the Bishop of Bangor, on the other hand, representing the view that forms of ceremonies in a church matter little, argued, as Macaulay after him, that the succession in any event was entirely uncertain and could not be relied on as a basis for a Church. Maddox, Bishop of Worcester, defended Episcopacy only as suited to the form of civil government in England and many other Latitudinarians were of his opinion.

The necessity of episcopal government if the Church of England was to be kept in being was shown by the practice of Wesley to ordain as he would on the ground that Episcopacy was first asserted "a divine right in the middle of Queen Elizabeth's reign". Very soon his followers themselves ordained ministers without any care for form or succession and eventually his whole movement left the Church, to form a great body of dissent.

So rapidly, however, did belief in the doctrine of succession falter in Georgian times that when early in the nineteenth century, before the Oxford Movement, Bishop Philpotts advanced it, it was considered a high church eccentricity, and in 1835 Manning caused some sensation by preaching on the succession at the Cathedral at Chichester. By Sidney Smith he was vehemently ridiculed. As the future Cardinal declared, "Our commission to witness for Christ hangs on this question, are the Bishops of our Church the successors in lineal descent of our Lord's apostles?" Later he was to answer that question in the negative, but that conclusion, and the later papal condemnation of Anglican succession on the ground of invalidity of the Sacrament of order and consecration, does not here directly concern us. The question may be asked, assuming the Church of England to be justified in its consecration service (which Catholics would deny), is the doctrine of succession a necessary part of the claim of the Anglican Church to be part of the Church universal? Anglicans as a whole have never decided the matter nor taken into full consideration the criticisms of Hatch and Lightfoot.

The matter may be said to be still open; thus, while any reunion with the Catholic Church (other than by submission) is not possible, a close alliance with other Protestant denominations is not only feasible but by many Anglicans desired. To that end, it appears, the Anglican Church may be willing to abandon her full claim to apostolic episcopal succession. So much may be gathered from the report on unity accepted by the Bishops at the last Lambeth Conference in 1948, which provides that in all future approaches to reunion:

"1. The theological issues, and especially those concerning the Church and the ministry, should be faced at the outset.

2. The unification of the ministry in a form satisfactory to all the bodies concerned, at the inauguration of the union or as soon as possible thereafter, is likely to be a prerequisite to success in all future proposals designed to secure the reunion of the Churches.

3. Any steps which may involve commitments in the way of union with non-Anglican Churches, or which would lead to the withdrawal of a portion of the Anglican Communion from our particular family of Churches should be approached with a sense of great responsi-

bility, and only after such consultation with other Churches of the Anglican Communion as the situation demands. The normal body for such consultation is the Lambeth Conference. In cases where action has to be taken urgently the Church or Province concerned should at least consult the Metropolitans of all the Anglican Churches or Provinces.

4. The integral connexion between the Church and the ministry should be safeguarded in all proposals for achieving intercommunion through the creation of a mutually recognised ministry. There is a danger that efforts to solve the problem of the ministry in detachment from the problem of the Church may lead to administrative and disciplinary confusion as well as theological ambiguities. The ministry is, in our view, an organ of Christ in His Body and can only function healthily in the Body. None of us hold that actual succession and correct formulae of ordination can guarantee a true and effectual episcopate or presbyterate apart from the faith and corporate life in which they are set."

*   *   *   *   *

If to be loved or feared is a criterion of individual vitality, the same consideration may surely be applied to institutions, secular or religious. Judged by such a standard, and it would seem to be a fair one, the Church of England, despite Conferences, Missions and attempted revivals, must be admitted to present to the outsider all the symptoms of advancing impotence. For several hundred years the majority of the English have allowed this Church to model their moral principles, while they, in their turn, have left an indelible impress upon their Church. Even those who broke away under the influence of some or other "enthusiasm", the Dissenters, have a kindly feeling for the State Church so long as its local behaviour is not too "high". The Wesleyans have described themselves as

non-conforming members of the Church of England; many
Dissenters are christened, married and buried by the National
Church; indeed, as parishioners, they are legally entitled to
these services. No law of mixed marriages curtails their freedom of choice in the religion of their spouse or the education
of their children. They share, for the most part, when young,
the instruction in undenominational religion prescribed by
Parliament and county syllabuses with their Anglican neigh-
bours. In all religious denominations, save the Catholic,
Modernism, often in a form which reduces Christianity to
decent moral precept, is at work ceaselessly undermining even
such foundations as are still precariously maintained in Creed,
Prayer Book and Articles. The distaste for dogmatic teaching
of any kind is even more harmful to the Nonconformist than
to the Anglican, for the former must justify his separation from
his National Church by some defined difference, such as a belief
in the verbal accuracy of the whole Bible, or a distaste for
Episcopacy, or reliance on the salvation of the elect, while the
Anglican may believe what he pleases, from the indefiniteness
of the Modern Churchman's Union to the almost ultra-Roman
observances of the extreme Anglo-Catholic.

Again, in matter of behaviour, the Puritan ideals of
Nonconformists no longer appeal to the present generation,
and the notion of the elect makes more appeal to the national-
ism of the people than to any theological superiority. From all
which considerations it would seem that the Church of
England, whatever may happen to the Anglo-Catholics, is
likely in the end to recover its lost Nonconformist element,
and so become more rather than less Protestant.[1]

That this is now the ideal and goal of many of the Bishops

---

[1] In the Convocation of Canterbury, the Archbishop recently said that "in
a sermon at Cambridge in 1946, he, fearing stalemate, made a suggestion for an
examination which, in essence, would lead to an acceptance by the Free Churches
of much which their own history and past experience had led them to repudiate
and resist. That was entirely his own suggestion, designed to reopen discussion,
and he was glad it had done so. There was not then, nor was there now, any
official policy of his, nor of anybody else, in these matters, and he had never
looked beyond the stage of discussions."

cannot be denied; a new international oecumenical, *Council of the Churches of the World*, has been established which makes pronouncements *urbi et orbi*, rarely mentioning the fact that the "great Latin Church of the West", as the Anglicans have officially labelled the Catholic Church, whether they do or do not agree with particular published opinions, is no part of their company.

The Anglo-Catholics are long suffering; the Jerusalem bishopric shared with Lutherans, the Gorham judgment denying the Catholic doctrine of Baptism as essential, the refusal of authority, save capriciously, to allow the liturgical adoration of the Blessed Sacrament, the toleration of heretical Bishops, the schemes for intercommunion with Dissenters in the Dominions, the official permission in certain cases for interchange of pulpits with Nonconformists, the vexatious petty legal proceedings against them ordering the removal of what they believe to be lawful ornaments, the appointment on the recommendation of a Prime Minister, who need not be Christian, of the members of the episcopal bench and the compulsion of Bishops under law to consecrate them, the continued recognition of the Crown as in ecclesiastical matters supreme governor—a power, in fact, now exercised by a Government the majority of which may be agnostic—the regulation of their prayers by parliamentary legislation or by rejection or approval of Church measures, all these and many more fetters and obligations inconsistent with their beliefs, many of which can only be expressed by breaking the law and therefore dependent on a cynical or indifferent tolerance, the recent knowledge that their reliance on the Catholic nature of their liturgy is unsound, the disquieting feeling that, at bottom, their beliefs and practices are without authority—all these facts have so far failed to shake the adherence of the majority who remain members of the Church of England and in communion with those whom they would admit disagree with them in everything save the minimum of Christian creed.

How long this state of affairs can continue cannot be foretold; disestablishment would probably hasten a crisis such as occurred in the days of Newman and Manning. It is the policy of the Bishops not unduly to disturb any of their diminishing flock, but the time must come when the laws of contradiction will no longer be able to be evaded; the division between incompatibles no longer to be averted. In any case it cannot be gainsaid that the Church of England has ceased to hold the mass of the English people; at best, to quote Mgr. Knox, it has become sectarian.

In the recent words of a not unsympathetic foreign observer:

"The Church of England is undergoing a very serious crisis. Since the war, religious practice has dropped very considerably. Indifference to religion and even the loss of moral sense have increased, particularly in the young generations. Anglicanism is suffering the fate of all the traditions. People were comfortably installed there, through force of habit. Rites, formulae, practice formed part of the even tenor of life but are out of fashion in a world which is restless and taken up with the struggle for money. It is unnecessary to emphasise this, for in every country of Europe the official religion or religion of the majority exhibits the same signs of old age and the same anachronism. But if one no longer finds the same vitality as formerly, one does find in the Church of England the same diversity and that is what strikes the observer at first sight. The Anglo-Catholics form a more homogeneous current than the others, with more uniformity in teaching and among theologians—the appearance of the report on 'Catholicity' seems to prove this. It can even be said that it is from their ranks that the majority of those who observe Sunday are recruited, and it is there that the greater number of theological works is found at the present time. But the other currents, Evangelicals, Liberals, which intermingle considerably, are important. The high church remains a minority among the faithful as a whole. It presents indeed a striking diversity, from the Papalists who are close to Rome and (Anglo) Catholics attached to the creeds, to complete compliance with the Prayer Book, to Tradition, but opposed to Rome.

An examination of the doctrine confirms this eternal diversity. Any dogmatic study of Anglicanism comes up against a major difficulty: the absence of an Anglican theology, at least in the sense in which we understand the term. If in the Catholic Church there are schools of thought, attempts to set forth and explain the truth in different systems, at any rate there is agreement upon the content of this truth. When one wants to know what the (Catholic) Church teaches, all that is necessary is to consult a good manual, Thomist or otherwise. There is no theology, there are only theologians. This does not mean that fantasy and arbitrariness are paramount, but there is no logical system of Anglican theology. There is no theology of, but only in the Church of England."

*   *   *   *   *

"Anglicanism, generally speaking, is not a system of religion, nor a body of truth, but a feeling," writes Mgr. Knox in his *Spiritual Aeneid*, but it is a feeling which has taken many forms. Thus while until recently it was thought that there were three main streams, the Evangelical, the Modernist, and what has been called the "Catholic", it appears, according to Dr. Wand, the Bishop of London, that in reality there are but two; for the "majority are content to modulate their Catholicism or Evangelicalism with varying degrees of liberal thought —Liberalism does not become Modernism until the possibility of miracle is denied!" At the present time, he admits, both sides seem to be pressed "as far as they will go within the limits of Anglican formularies".

"From the beginning of our separate history there has been a certain tension between those who emphasised the old Catholic traditions of the Church and others who

M*

stressed more strongly the different aspects of religious truth believed to have been recovered at the Reformation,"

he concludes in his final essay in the symposium *The Anglican Communion*.

In this issue, were we to confine our attention to the formularies of the Anglican Church, as finally established in the reign of Elizabeth, both as to its doctrine as revealed in the thirty-nine Articles, Homilies, and Prayer Book, and as to its monarchical secular constitution, to be found in the Statutes of Supremacy and Uniformity, or in the prerogative powers of the Crown as shown in Advertisements, regulations and Articles to Bishops ordering them under royal authority to regulate and define doctrine and ceremonial, there can really be no serious doubt that the Elizabethan Church was both Protestant (whether Lutheran or Calvinist or a mixture of both may be debated) and Erastian—that is, under the supreme governorship of the Crown.

The state of affairs, though it may have been modified in practice, has not officially been altered. Still by Article 37 of the Articles of Religion, to which even now Anglican clergy must give general assent, "the Queen hath the chief power, unto whom all estates ecclesiastical doth appertain". Still the Crown orders the election of diocesan Bishops through the writ of *congé d'élire*, having but "colours, shadows or pretences of elections, serving nevertheless to no purpose", as a statute of Edward VI put it, and still Parliament has full power, directly or indirectly, to veto any measure to change or enact any law to affect the doctrine, ceremonial or other ecclesiastical matter. It was this overriding secular power which caused Dr. Hensley Henson, the Bishop of Durham, after the rejection of the Prayer Book Measure by Parliament, to advocate disestablishment as the "only way out of the impasse". His fellow Bishops did not agree with him and the position remains as it was at the time of the Elizabethan settlement when a Bishop truly said "we are under authority and cannot make any innovation without the sanction of the Queen".

Thus on all counts the Protestants may be said to have established their case. How then is it that so many high church Anglicans repudiate their own formularies or endeavour to evade them? According to the historian Lecky, from the time of the Revolution "it became a settled maxim of English politics that government is intended solely to promote the civil and temporal interests of the Community; that the salvation of souls is not within its functions". Yet the secular legislature still endows the Anglican Church with pecular privileges and allows it to retain much pre-reformation Catholic property, though Tests at Universities and for public appointments (save that of the Lord Chancellor) have been abolished. A Bishop of the Church of England may yet enjoy certain legislative rights, he may still be a Peer Spiritual and vote, if eligible, in the House of Lords, while the clergy have the disqualification of not sitting in the Commons;[1] it may well be asked, why, when the Church of England's practising membership is probably not a twentieth of the nation, these things should still abide?

That there is no necessary connection between the system of Establishment and sanctity is shown by the state of the Episcopacy in the eighteenth century, when Nonconformists had no more protection than that given by the Toleration Acts and Catholics none at all.

The cynical division of Bishops into two kinds, those of "business" for men of ability, and those of "ease" for those of family and fashion by Grenville, the Prime Minister, in the mid-eighteenth century, had no canonical sanction, it is true, but testifies to the low opinion of Episcopacy at the time. The case of Archbishop Moore, it is hoped, is not typical. He was asked by the Duchess of Marlborough on her widowhood himself to marry her but, writes a contemporary commentator, without a hint of satire:

"From a strong principle of honour, Mr. Moore

[1] A disability recently reasserted in the case of an Irish cleric by the Privy Council.

declined the advantage of the connection, and so sensible was the succeeding Duke of the generosity of his conduct that as the first token of his gratitude he settled upon him an annuity of £400 and rapidly obtained for him very valuable Church preferment."

A Durham Prebend and the Deanery of Canterbury were followed by the Bishopric of Bangor and, on the death of Archbishop Cornwallis, Moore was appointed to Canterbury in 1783.

Again, Dr. Ollard in his history of the Oxford Movement relates how Dr. John Douglas was Bishop from 1787 to 1807. His chaplain examined a candidate for Ordination while he (the chaplain) was shaving, and stopped the examination when the candidate had construed two words. An example of the qualifications exacted by such Bishops from their Ordination candidates is on record in another case. In 1822 George Spencer, son of the Lord Spencer of the day, was to be ordained in order to take the family living. He applied to the Bishop of Peterborough, and wrote to the examining chaplain to know what books he would have to read. That gentleman replied: "As far as I am concerned, in my character of examiner, it is impossible that I could entertain any idea of subjecting a gentleman of whose talents I am acquainted to any examination except as a matter of form."

Dr. Garbett, Archbishop of York, who defends Establishment, nevertheless deplores the fact that "the industrial revolution was a period when the Church failed to see and to denounce the appalling sufferings of the poor in the factories and the mines". While, however, today the Anglican Church, or some part of it, does speak on international, social or economic problems, the Archbishop frankly admits that the Catholic and Free Churches have also so spoken. "From time to time," he adds, "the different churches have made united statements on great international or domestic subjects." He cites as an example in his *Church and State in England* a case where the "two Archbishops, Cardinal Hinsley and the leaders of the

Free Churches united in support of a declaration of the Pope on the necessary conditions of world peace".

But this unity of effort on specific matters—raising no doctrinal problems—has not extended sufficiently to bring the discordant elements in the Church of England together or to resolve their differences.

Thus, the late Mr. Sidney Dark, an Anglo-Catholic editor of the *Church Times*, declared that if "the English Church is the Catholic Church in England, it must possess an Apostolic Ministry, the claims of the Church depend on its possession of a divinely authorised and divinely commissioned ministry, inheriting the ghostly privileges entrusted by our Lord to His Apostles. Without such a Ministry there can be no Eucharist. Without such a Ministry there can be no Church." The same writer stresses that Dr. Headlam, the Bishop of Gloucester, thinks Episcopacy to be "a mere matter of convenience". Nor does Mr. Dark in his book, *Anglo-Catholicism*, hesitate to call one of his Fathers in God a heretic!

The fact (regretted by Anglo-Catholics but approved warmly by Anglican Evangelicals and, curiously, by some Nonconformists) is that, in the last resort, the formularies and doctrine of the Church of England, as much of its higher personnel, are fixed by the Crown, acting through Parliament or its Ministers of State. As Mgr. Moyes wrote in 1891, and his words come with greater force today after the rejection by Parliament of two Prayer Books approved by the Anglican Bishops, by Convocation and the Assembly:

"Caesar (who today is the secular Executive Legislature and Judiciary) is to the Church of England her supreme governor upon earth. He rules her. He confirms her laws. He, in final instance, determines the formularies of belief and worship to be used in her Churches. He is final Court of Appeal in all her causes. He appoints her Bishops. Practically, it is for him to say what she shall teach, and whom she shall employ to teach it. The Reformation and the legislation of Henry VIII, Edward VI and Elizabeth are the concrete application of the principle. Quite true Caesar does not become a clergyman. He does not administer the Eucharist. And the jest of Francis I that he expected every morning to hear that his brother the King of England (Henry VIII) had sung High Mass, was after all quite superfluous. But he appoints the one who does celebrate the Eucharist, and decides the words and way in which he shall administer it. He does not mount into the pulpit. But he fixes the limits of doctrine inside which the preacher must keep when he gets there. If he finds that certain men do not preach a given doctrine, or follow a given policy, he can appoint others who will. As long as he can man the Sees he can always tune the Episcopate and the pulpits. Nor does it sensibly better the case to plead that in doing all this Caesar invariably takes the advice of his Churchmen. It would be surprising if he did not. But throughout the entire movement of Church government, Caesar it is who does it. It is he who is at work. It is, in the long run, his will and his word that say and seal and lend effective validity to the whole proceeding. He is the motive power of the Church machinery."

Of these great powers of the Sword over the Anglican Keys, by far the most important today lies in the effectual authority of the Prime Minister to appoint Bishops. After the experience of the Prayer Books (and the Bishops' subsequent repudiation of the rejection of the books in the permission accorded to the clergy by their Ordinaries in their "administrative discretion to be guided by the proposals set forth in the 1928 book"), Parliament is unlikely again to interfere in matters to which a modern House of Commons is becoming increasingly indifferent, but with episcopal nominations it is different. The tendency of the Assembly has been to put ever more power into the hands of the Archbishops and their suffragans, and the clergy are rapidly losing that independence which formerly was associated with their "freehold". It follows that whoever selects the Bench in effect controls the behaviour and, to an extent, the kind of beliefs and practices which the Church of England will be encouraged to support.

Historically the royal interference with the election of Bishops dates from very early times. After the Norman conquest, and particularly in the thirteenth century and after, while the Crown might nominate, the papal bull of Canonical institution was necessary, and, in the case of Archbishops, the *rallium*, before a Bishop was lawfully able to exercise his functions. The opinion of Dr. Garbett that "in substance the change at the Reformation was unimportant" is one which no reformer at that time would have accepted. He admits that before the statute of 1534 ultimate papal control had superseded the election by chapter and confirmation by the Metropolitans. In reality the breach with the Catholic Church was, as it was intended to be, complete, in that, before the Reformation, for many centuries no man could be a Bishop without canonical approval from Rome, whoever had appointed him. If Dr. Garbett is right, St. Thomas Moore and St. John Fisher vainly suffered martyrdom.

But to pass from early history; even in the days of Queen Victoria, Lord Salisbury in more than one appointment had overridden her desires, yet her observation that promotion of Bishops seemed to "hamper their freedom of speech" is shrewd. Indeed it must be admitted that in the Anglican Church Bishops have often been chosen rather for their discretion and mediocrity than as apostles. Dr. Garbett comments on Mr. Ramsay MacDonald, a Presbyterian, that "he had been well served by his secretariat". This system of political appointment, the capitular confirmation being a formality and in any case ordered by the Crown, is said by the present Archbishop of York to have "certain advantages", but he admits the dangers to be great. He remarks how the Prime Minister today need not be a Christian or even a believer in God. The fact that Bishops are legislators also has been taken into account in the past as late as the time of Disraeli, and Dr. Westcott was objected to by Lord Salisbury because of his "socialist tendencies". Dr. Garbett admits that today "a Bishop has comparatively little influence except among the faithful of his flock; and when he speaks is probably unreported" and so, he fears, little care may be taken by Prime Ministers in the future except in the case of a few senior Sees. His remedy would be apparently to consult the Chapters before the Premier advises an appointment. "To ask for the transfer of appointment from the Crown to a college of Bishops (as is the case in the Eastern churches) would in effect be a demand for disestablishment." This, differing from Dr. Henson in his later years, Evangelical churchmen oppose. At their conference in 1951 they declared that:

"We affirm our conviction that the historic alliance between Church and State, known as the Establishment, remains God's will for England. We pledge ourselves to support it, welcoming all efforts to adapt the Establishment more fully to modern conditions and needs.

The continuance of the royal supremacy, as constitutionally exercised through Parliament, is not inconsistent with the spiritual autonomy of the Church. It is a supremacy of jurisdiction, not of direction or initiation. As a safeguard of order it does not hinder but rather assists the Church in the maintenance of its spiritual function and prophetic witness.

It belongs to the exercise of the royal supremacy to ensure that the laity are granted full rights in all matters pertaining to the Church, including the making of canons ecclesiastical and other Church laws. We recommend that legislation necessary to secure this end be initiated."

By missives, mandates and other legal documents and compulsions the Crown orders the Dean and Chapter of a diocese to appoint such Bishop as the principal politician in power wills! The Bishop-elect still swears that "Your Majesty is the only supreme Governor of this realm in spiritual and ecclesiastical things, as well as in temporal . . . and that no foreign prelate or potentate has any jurisdiction in this realm"

—the oath of allegiance. To a Protestant, discounting the powers of Bishops, this may mean little, but, to quote Canon Lacey: "When Anglo-Catholics say that the Church of England must conform to the faith and practice of the whole Catholic Church, they are referring to the one episcopate of the organic church." To such the election of Bishops by compulsion of statesmen without any final spiritual control, papal or metropolitan, must be disquieting. It is doubtful, from their standpoint, whether a consultation prior to appointment with the chapters would supply the remedy. In considering the status and authority of the Lambeth Conferences, it should be borne in mind that few Bishops, outside England, are Crown appointments, so that here, as in so many other matters, hesitancy and confusion are only too sadly evident.

Confronted with these disunities and diversities of opinion implicit in Anglicanism, two recent formulations of belief were compiled for and at the request of the present Archbishop of Canterbury, each of which contains a preface by that high ecclesiastic. One, *The Fulness of Christ*,[1] an evangelical production (1950), states unambiguously that "We believe that the Reformation rediscovery of the doctrine of Justification by Faith alone is a central and crucial part of the gospel. It is as fundamental to the doctrine of salvation as are the Nicene and Chalcedonian statements to the doctrine of the Person of Christ . . . we believe that the 'protestant' insight into the nature of namely, that it is ' a congregation of faithful men, in the God and with each other in Christ, a fellowship which comes into being and grows as men respond in faith to the gospel presented to them in word and sacraments', is a fundamental truth, the recognition of which is essential in a reunited Church. This truth could be safeguarded by a definition of the visible Church such as that contained in Article XIX, namely

[1] The following are the authors: S. F. Allison, H. Chadwick, F. D. Coggan, S. L. Greenslade, D. E. W. Harrison, H. G. G. Herklots, G. H. G. Hewitt, J. P. Hickinbotham, G. W. H. Lampe, C. F. D. Moule, S. C. Neill, W. M. F. Scott, E. Steinly, F. J. Taylor, P. Thornton-Duesbery, M. A. C. Warren and R. R. Williams.

that it is a congregation of faithful men, in the which the pure Word of God is preached, and the Sacraments be duly ministered according to Christ's ordinance in all those things that of necessity are requisite to the same."

On the other hand, the more high church publication *Catholicity*[1] asserts that:

"The first of the two radical errors of Luther is, then, the dissociation of Justification from the doctrine of Creation: the second is that of Justification from Sanctification . . . It is not enough to appeal, as the reformers (and the authority of the *Fulness of Christ*) appealed, to 'the Bible' or 'the Gospel'. It is necessary, in appealing to the Bible, to appeal also to the Tradition of the primitive Church as the context in which the Bible had its origin and meaning. And it is necessary, in appealing to the Gospel, to remember that the Gospel involved a series of historical events, an interpretation of those events, and an apostolate commissioned with authority to teach both the history and its true interpretation. It is grievously misleading to appeal to Bible or Gospel without appealing also to the apostolic Church as the witness and keeper of both; and a distorted form of appeal to Christian beginnings underlies the eclipse of the doctrine of the Authority of the Church amongst Protestants."

Very many other disagreements could be cited from these two writings—in fact, on many essentials they are directly at variance, and to them must be added a third school, the "Modernists", who, however, have not yet prepared a companion volume to add to the confusion. "Like Protestantism and Catholicism," write the authors of *Catholicity*, "Liberalism has its avowed adherents."

[1] *A Study in the Conflict of Christian Traditions in the West*, being a Report presented to His Grace the Archbishop of Canterbury: E. S. Abbott, H. J. Carpenter, V. A. Demant, Gregory Dix, T. S. Eliot, A. M. Farrer, F. W. Green, A. G. Hebert, R. C. Mortimer, A. M. Ramsey, A. Reeves, C. H. Smyth, the Bishop of Southampton and L. S. Thornton.

Of some modern churchmen, the same Anglo-Catholics declare that

"God is presented as the loving Father, conceived after our own notions of love and without a word about the Divine Judgment. The great events of the Gospel are affirmed, but so robbed of their apostolic interpretation that Redemption is equated with the movement of spiritual progress within history, and Resurrection with the ability of good men to survive death. A severing of the New Testament from the Old undermines the duo-testamentary basis of the faith, banishes the continuity of the Church as the Israel of God, stultifies the relation of Law and Gospel and sentimentalises the doctrine of God. This debased teaching finds its way into official pronouncements, sermons, hymn-books and classrooms."

Yet these "Liberals" have an honoured place in the Anglican Church, several have been, or are, Bishops, though some have denied, without any action officially taken against them, fundamental tenets of the Christian faith.

It is the custom of most Anglican apologists, faced with this indisputable ambiguity of belief and failure of authority which exists in their communion to justify their position by declaring that it is peculiarly suited to the temperament of Englishmen, who, it is said, are suspicious of exact reasoning or clerical definition, but such an attitude towards matters of eternal significance discloses a secular and pragmatic outlook which, though possibly defensible in the field of politics or diplomacy, is quite irreconcilable with the great claims of the Christian religion to treat Man in his relation to God as a matter of infinite moment, far outreaching any national, racial or territorial considerations. Ritual may express itself in various ways according to the particular mentality and spiritual development of a people—the Catholic Church has several rites but one principle—but belief in the Gospels and the Creeds is one not to be tortured to suit

individual or even national requirements—for Faith is something other than modes of exposition, and the Church of
England must sooner or later face the question: If in the
future it is to be regarded, what in fact does it teach or believe?

This inescapable requirement of certainty is a comparatively new problem for the National Church; in the days of its
foundation nothing is more clear than the insistence of its
political authors on the need for unqualified acceptance of its
statutory theology—the "Articles" of Henry VIII and the
Acts of Uniformity of Edward VI and Elizabeth show this
very clearly; little was heard in these days of "comprehensiveness" or "modern interpretation". We know now that the
"primitive church", sought by those monarchs and their
Bishops and statesmen, never had any existence—that the
farther we go back into history the more evident becomes the
fact of the belief in a mystical corporate Church, founded by
Christ Himself, and in the sacrament of the altar as the occasion
for the meeting and redemption of the Faithful. It is over
fifteen hundred years ago that the cry at a Council, still
acknowledged by Anglicans, "Peter has spoken", accepted the
Papal right to declare the Faith. We may discard the Catholic
assumptions, if we will, as out of date, but not on the ground of
their inconsistency with an imagined primitive Church; that
however was the main ground of the Reformers. By modern
Anglicans (and even other Protestants) the individualistic
notion of an uncatholic, unsacramental primitive Church has
been discarded as historically and theologically indefensible.

Thus we see how today the Anglican Church, be it
justified or not, has departed from the beliefs of its founders
—no longer does it assert that salvation depends on Faith
alone, and in reality, though not by admission, is more inclined
to look to the Council of Trent for authority on this matter.

So also, that fundamental acceptance by the reformers of
the inherent depravity of man has been abandoned, so also the
belief of the Calvinists—and Cranmer in his later years when
he drew the Liturgy was one—in Predestinarianism and the
saving of the elect. On the other hand the Reformation has

deprived the Anglican Church, among other ideas, of the notion of Sanctifying Grace, or indeed of any exact knowledge of the nature of Grace at all. It has discouraged natural and scholastic theology, so that many of its ministers are wholly ignorant of the teachings of the Christian neo-platonists, the scholastics, or even the later researches of Gilson, Mercier or Maritain. Their own scholars, Thornton, Mascall and Farrer, for example, are appreciated only by a select few. Purgatory[1] has been eliminated and the sublime ideal of the Beatific Vision lost.

That in fact there is no authority in a Church which still accords to Bishops an efficient supervisory power is evident. Many Anglo-Catholics, themselves accepting the Catholic principle that they are but delegates of their Bishops, disobey their Fathers in God without any apparent ecclesiastical anxiety, and the low church party, when their Bishops show "Catholic leanings", ignore them also.

Yet Episcopalianism, we are told, is the principal thing which at present prevents a union between the Anglicans and other Protestant bodies in England—it is very confusing!

In the words of Dr. Gregg, Anglican Primate of All Ireland, after the Lambeth Conference of 1948:

> "I am not sure if a good deal of this laxity of conviction is not to be traced to the very dangerous suggestion which has been current for some twenty years past, to the effect that, while the acceptance of episcopacy as a practice is indispensable for those who would enter into communion with the Anglican Church, no particular theory of episcopacy need be insisted on. I regard this view as both unsound and unprincipled. It seems to me nothing less than the rankest ritualism. To urge the acceptance of an institution without insisting on any reasoned meaning of it reduces it, in my opinion, to something like mumbo-jumbo. To have no philosophy of the institution which

---

[1] Of Purgatory, Sir William Joynson Hicks (Lord Brentford) said, "I have no use for it." The question, commented G. K. Chesterton, should rather have been put, "What use has Purgatory for Joynson Hicks?"

episcopacy is, is to undermine the Ordinal, which insists
on episcopal ordination, and to leave it to be supposed
that this insistence rests only on antiquarian pedantry or
sectarian prejudice."

Commenting on a definition of Episcopacy designed to
satisfy Dissenters at the conference on *Church Relations in
England in 1950*, the Anglo-Catholic Church Union declared:

"It appears that the Anglican attitude to episcopacy
implied by them is one that Free Churchmen, if fully conscious of it, would find very hard to accept. The only way
of reassuring them would seem to be to explain that the
Anglican insistence on episcopacy did not really represent
a coherently thought-out position at all but was merely a
concession on the part of the authorities of the Church of
England to the prejudices of those Anglicans who believe
episcopacy to be essential to the Church's existence. The
Church of England would in effect be saying to the Free
Churchmen, 'We agree with you that episcopacy is really a
thing indifferent, but for the sake of peace and unity within
the Church of England we must ask you to accept it'."

And, further, that

"The Archbishop of Canterbury himself, in his Cambridge sermon, emphasized that one of the objections to
reunion schemes of the 'constitutional' type arises from
the unresolved tensions within the Church of England
itself. 'When it is thus engaged in a delicate task,' His Grace
pointed out, 'it is unwise at the same time to involve it in
questions of constitutional affiliation to other denominations.'"

At a public meeting on January 30, 1951, the Archbishop
of Canterbury said: "The Anglican Communion, with its
fellowship of Churches, has a special responsibility at this time
in the world. We have no doctrine of our own—we only
possess the Catholic doctrine of the Catholic Church, en-
shrined in the Catholic Creeds; and those creeds we hold

without addition or diminution. We stand firm on that rock."

To this the Anglo-Catholic Council replied:

"We believe this statement to represent the fundamental truth about the Church of England, as of other Churches of the Anglican Communion. We are, therefore, unable to assent to the procedure outlined in the report—*Church Relations in England*—or to the actions frequently taken which blur the distinctions between the Church of England and the non-episcopal communions.

We could never agree to be in communion with bodies which will not express their faith by the recitation of the Catholic Creeds in their worship.

We are unable to treat the question of the ministry as if it were not involved in the Catholic faith as a whole, and were only a question of Church order. We believe that the Church of England is committed by her formularies to the acceptance of apostolic authority for the threefold order of bishops, priests, and deacons; and that no other form of ministry can be regarded as the equivalent of this.

We cannot agree that confirmation should be regarded as an optional rite which may or may not be accepted before admission to Holy Communion at our altars.

We believe that either the reunion of, or intercommunion between, the Church of England and a body that remained wholly or partly non-episcopal in its ministry would involve discarding the theological basis of episcopacy to which the Church of England is committed.

We do not believe that unity is furthered by holding joint services in churches, by inviting nonconformist preachers to occupy our pulpits, or by proposals for intercommunion with non-episcopal bodies. In many cases, services have been held and proposals made which go far beyond both the letter and the spirit of the Regulations of Convocation made in 1943."

Despite the persistent opposition of Bishops and clergy in the past, all governmental, military and learned professions are now open regardless of creed (save that a Catholic apparently is still precluded from being Lord Chancellor); and there is little left, but the possession of Churches and emoluments and the conduct of civic ceremonial services, to show that the Anglican Church is any more the Church of the Nation than is any other denomination.[1] The truth is that, judged by any profession of religion, the great majority of English people are more or less agnostic, and very many not even baptised.[2] So we leave the matter; pragmatic hesitancy and want of clarity have proved, it would appear, less ingratiating than has been claimed. Whether people accept or reject a Church, they at least wish to know what it teaches and what it demands of them in their lives. In the case of the Church of England, it may well be that, at long last, ambiguity will no longer be found to afford an abiding foundation, in faith or in reason.

> *"Thus many a youth I've known set out,*
> *Half Protestant, half Papist,*
> *And rambling long the world about,*
> *Turn infidel or atheist."*[3]

THE END

[1] This fact was recently deplored by Dr. Mortimer, Bishop of Exeter, at an Anglo-Catholic rally when he declared that: "One of the most surprising and distressing developments of the last century has been the tendency to look on the Church of England as only one among many Christian denominations. The Church has been progressively thrown back to an apologetic and defensive attitude."

[2] According to a recent report of the National Assembly, 95 per cent of the population do not attend any place of worship on Sunday (the *Book of Uncommon Prayer*, Moyle, 1950). Of those who attend at least half are Catholic or Nonconformist. According to Mr. Gorer, who recently conducted an enquiry for *The People*:

> "Only a quarter of today's parents do not teach their children to say their prayers or hear anything about religion. But of the other three-quarters, only a minority, a quarter at most, go to church themselves. The Catholic position is bad enough, that nearly half the Catholics miss Sunday Mass, but they make the best showing—with Baptists and Congregationalists next, producing a third of their members who go every week. Within the Church of England, writes Mr. Gorer, 'the position is frankly appalling; just one in ten is a regular churchgoer, and nearly half never enter a church at all'; while less than half say any daily prayers."

[3] Pope's *Miscellanies*.